A Mind Ordir

My Experience of Living with Anorexia and Schizoaffective Disorder

Dr Tanya J Sheldon

To Dr McDonnell,
with love
+ thanks.

chipmunkapublishing

the mental health publisher

All rights reserved, no part of this publication may be reproduced by any means, electronic, mechanical photocopying, documentary, film or in any other format without prior written permission of the publisher.

Published by

Chipmunkapublishing

PO Box 6872

Brentwood

Essex CM13 1ZT

United Kingdom

http://www.chipmunkapublishing.com

Copyright © Dr Tanya J Sheldon 2011

Chipmunkapublishing gratefully acknowledge the support of Arts Council England.

Author Biography

Born in 1982, Dr Tanya J Sheldon has the unusual distinction of having taken her finals and graduated from medical school whilst detained in a psychiatric institution. Diagnosed with anorexia at 17, she recovered, only to become ill again several years later with schizoaffective disorder, an illness which causes abnormally high and low moods, as well as detachment from reality. Having been sectioned three times in the UK, she has made progress since undergoing intensive treatment in the United States. No longer permitted to practise medicine, Dr Sheldon is studying to become a Clinical Educator, enjoys creative writing, and volunteers for two mental health charities.

Dr Tanya J Sheldon

Dedicated to my aunt,

without whose support I would not have been around to write this book.

Dr Tanya J Sheldon

Foreword

By Dr Stuart Flanagan

Mental Health has become a much discussed topic in recent years, with very welcome campaigns from charities outlining how common mental illness is, and the importance of keeping our minds, as well as our bodies, fit. As a doctor myself, I'm well aware of the need for a holistic approach in managing my patients, and try to be sensitive to the discrimination against those suffering with mental health problems, and the difficulties they can face because of them.

But it wasn't until I read "A Mind Less Ordinary" that I became aware of some of my own preconceptions, and lack of clarity on what being mentally ill really means. What does it really feel like to see no future? What does it feel like be closed in by your own thoughts? How do you cope when you see the world differently from everyone else in your life?

This book offers a unique insight into experiences that are commonly diagnosed by psychiatrists, but are rarely described by those who endure them. Tanya's unique position of having been both patient and doctor, of having experienced both sides of the bed, allows her to give voice to the person behind the psychiatric label.

We all suffer from mental issues to some small degree at various times in our lives, whether it's the anguish of bereavement, the stress of exams or the lack of self-confidence in teenage years. Many of us have to face periods when we can't shake those feelings off. What if you couldn't really describe your mood, searching in vain for an explanation where there is none? What if you started feeling there really was no point?

Tanya has walked down those dark alleys of the mind. She has been to places that many of us cannot contemplate, and in our ignorance we dismiss. For others they are places that resonate strongly – feelings of isolation and lack of control. Fortunately for us she has come back to tell us exactly how she felt. Because that's what's missing from so much of our understanding of mental illness – what does it feel like? Only by understanding Tanya's experiences can we truly empathise with her and the many other people in our lives dealing with similar thoughts, though we may not be aware of it.

Tanya's courageous book is a unique insight into how we deal with mental health – as a society, and from my own point of view, as healthcare providers.

Mental illness is extremely challenging – to individuals, their healthcare providers, and to society as a whole. But the real challenge is changing all our minds – freeing them of prejudice and judgement. Allowing us to recognise there are good days as well as bad, and that we have brothers and sisters in society who are vulnerable and need our support. "A Mind Less Ordinary" is a powerful and important book that encourages celebrating the person behind the diagnosis.

Dr Stuart Flanagan Biography

Dr Stuart Flanagan is the resident Doctor on BBC Radio 1's Surgery. He is a regular contributor to various TV and radio shows including BBC Breakfast, Newsround and Radio 4. He is also an NHS Specialty Doctor in London and is involved in hosting the Royal College of Psychiatrists' annual World Mental Health Day.

Away from his stethoscope he enjoys cinema, indie music and following Liverpool FC.

Dr Tanya J Sheldon

Contents

1. Let Me Introduce Myself
2. Anorexia: Where it all Began
3. Depression
4. Self-Harm
5. Overdosing
6. Hypomania
7. Psychosis
8. Hospital
9. Treatment
10. Recovery?

Dr Tanya J Sheldon

Chapter 1

Let Me Introduce Myself

Let me introduce myself. I am 28 years old. I live on my own in an apartment but I have family and friends nearby, and until recently I had the company of a very noble hamster, who sadly succumbed to heart failure at the age of two. He is irreplaceable, but I will get another one soon. I like to have life around me.

I find that I am interested in almost everything, but I have a particular passion for the arts. I love watching foreign language films on DVD or at the local art-house cinema, sinking myself into a soft chair and allowing myself to be carried away by a quirky or intense storyline. I love to listen to music of all genres from Irish traditional via folk-rock to indie-pop. I enjoy classical sounds too, but I prefer to experience those in person - my favourite Friday evening activity involves buying a last-minute student ticket to hear the local orchestra. I play a few instruments as well. The piano was the first I learnt and, whilst I can no longer play to Grade 8 standard as I did at school, I can easily while away an hour or two tinkling the keys of my digital Yamaha. I own a guitar and violin, but I am a wind player at heart and I love to improvise on my flute or tin whistle. The theatre and an occasional art gallery visit are also treats for me, and I have also been known to frequent the opera. I am drawn to anything which offers an outward expression of the human soul.

I love the outdoors too. Getting out for a walk in the countryside or by the sea brings freshness to my outlook, and the serene beauty of the green landscape which surrounds my city enthrals me. I no longer play sport, but I still get a buzz from standing in the crowd at a rugby match. Indoors, I do yoga for relaxation, and from time to time I enjoy swimming at a local leisure centre, the gentle rhythm of the breast-stroke helping to soothe my body and mind. I shop for fun as well, and I have my own distinct style, preferring funky dresses to jeans or 'work-wear'.

I am also interested in the more concrete details of human life. I follow current affairs avidly and I enjoy being involved in local politics. I volunteer regularly in the constituency office of my own MP, and I can be found surveying the electorate throughout the year and canvassing come campaign time. Being a doctor, I am particularly interested in the politics of health and illness, and I have been involved both in individual health-related casework and in advising politicians on wider medical issues. I am also a 'Media Volunteer' and activist for a local mental health charity and the national organisation, Rethink, offering my time to talk to journalists and organisations who want to learn more about mental illness.

You see, I suffer from schizoaffective disorder, a condition which lies on a spectrum between schizophrenia and bipolar disorder (formerly known as manic depression). I also previously suffered from anorexia nervosa; however, I wanted to tell you some other important things about me first because – as I always say when I give a media interview – there is more to me than mental illness. I do not identify myself as 'a schizoaffective'. No, first and foremost, I am a young woman with interests and abilities, friends and relationships; a young woman who has been through good times and bad; a young woman who has succeeded in some things and failed in others; a young woman who has certain idiosyncrasies, but who is - in many ways - much like any other.

I have always written. I love to write. For me it is freeing and also grounding. I can let my imagination run wild in a work of fiction; I can try to contain my raging thoughts by committing them to paper. Throughout my illness, I have written much. It has not always made sense; with hindsight, my analysis of situations has often been flawed. But none of what I have written until now has ever been suitable for publication. Too many people are identifiable; too many of my loved ones could be hurt. This book is designed to be different. My purpose in writing it is not to display fine prose, nor to provoke sympathy. It is by no means a misery memoir. Instead, it is intended to help people who have not experienced mental illness to understand what it actually feels like from the inside. I invite you, in reading this, to step inside my head. A dangerous thing, indeed! Yet one which I hope will be enlightening.

There is no real chronology here. Some chapters relate to specific times in my life; most are more like essays, descriptions of my experience of particular symptoms over time. Many psychiatrists have written about the 'phenomenology' of mental illness, but few of them have actually lived through it as I have done. I cannot say that my experience will reflect that of every person with anorexia or schizoaffective disorder, or other related diagnoses, but I have spent a lot of time with fellow patients and have found in conversation that we have a lot in common. Many have urged me to tell my story – their story – whilst I have the capacity and motivation. I hope that I will do them justice.

Chapter 2

Anorexia: Where it all Began

I don't know why it stuck in my head, for at the time it had no reason to – a conversation with my dad as he drove me to school when I was around 13 years old. On the radio, the presenters were discussing the rise of something called 'anorexia', where people – mostly young girls – refused to eat. My dad turned to me and said, "Don't you ever do that, OK?" I laughed back at him, "You have no need to fear – I love my food far too much!" I genuinely believed myself.

It was true that I loved my food. I was no gastronome, but I was what was usually termed a 'big eater'. I had to be. I was playing sport all year round, training twice on most days, and I needed fuel. My mum would send me a Twix or a Mars bar for my break and I'd eat that and then go to the canteen for a doughnut as well. And I ate two hot dinners every day without thinking twice about it. I weighed about 9 stone, maybe a little more, which was entirely appropriate for an athlete of my height, though I only know this because we were occasionally weighed in school – for a science project, for example. I never thought of stepping on to the scales at home.

I can't remember exactly how things changed. It certainly wasn't sudden, and there wasn't one identifiable cause, but there are things which happened in my Lower 6th form year which seemed to contribute. In my mind, the most important of these was the fact that I had to stop playing sport. My left heel and ankle area had been giving me pain whilst playing hockey for some time, but it had always eased afterwards so I tended to forget about it until I started the next match or training session. Then one day, in February 1999, I ran out on to the pitch for the warm up and my ankle gave way. The pain was so bad that I could barely limp back to the changing rooms. I sat there weeping. It was as if I had a premonition that I wouldn't play hockey again. If I did, it was correct.

Something else from around this time sticks in my memory. I was in geography class one day when the teacher arrived late. She excused herself, saying that there had been Pavlova in the staff room and that she couldn't resist having some before coming round. This particular teacher happened to be a hockey player – a former English international, in fact – and I held her in high esteem. She went on to comment, "I love my food. If I stopped playing hockey, I'd balloon!" My brain made connections. 'I can't play hockey already. I eat a lot. Maybe I will balloon. I'd hate that.' I made a mental note to be more careful.

Lower 6th was also a difficult year for me because I began to experience certain thoughts and feelings which I had never had before. Mostly they emerged when I was thinking about what career I would follow and what university course to choose - my future plans in general. I began to realise that, whilst I was relatively content in the present – aside from the frustration of not being able to play the sports I loved – I had problems thinking ahead. There were practical issues in that my A Levels were varied and gave me lots of options; I was good at pretty much everything I did academically, and I wasn't sure what to pursue. But there was a much more real, and yet surreal, problem: All I could see when I looked forward was a kind of void. For the first time, I had the impression that there was some kind of dark presence with me, and I was scared. I began to make decisions based on what might help me feel safer instead of what

I was passionate about. And I seemed to be losing my passion in any case.

The next specific event that I remember is telling my mum that I was going to start 'eating more healthily'. I wasn't keeping fit through sport any more, I'd learnt a lot about nutrition in GCSE Physical Education, and I wanted to keep my body in good shape. I told her that, from then on, I would make myself up a lunch box, and I might not always eat her puddings. Mum had been on many diets and seemed quite impressed with my resolve. She knew that I needed to make adjustments to my previously sport-filled lifestyle and there was certainly nothing in my initial behaviour to concern her.

It began innocently. I substituted fruit for my break-time biscuits and cakes, packed wholemeal or wheaten bread sandwiches, and yoghurt for dessert. Essentially, all I was doing was following public health recommendations. But I have never been the sort of person to do things by halves, and gradually I introduced more changes – less ham in the sandwich, low fat yoghurt, no butter on the bread... And I became so dedicated to my new regime that I refused to go with my other packed-lunch regulars to the canteen for chips on Fridays. I was also relieved over time to discover that I could tolerate low impact exercise such as walking and swimming, and I began to plan this into my schedule.

And I felt better - much better, in fact. The dark thoughts and feelings gave way to a kind of euphoria, I was more alert in class, I seemed to need less sleep, and not being able to play sport did not bother me as much. People commented that my skin was glowing and clearer than ever, and that my eyes seemed brighter. I told them that it was all down to making healthy choices. It was almost as if I had discovered the elixir of life.

But it could not last. I thought that I was more in control of my life than ever; the reality was that anorexia was beginning to control me. My 'healthy choices' soon became unhealthy compulsions, but whenever I realised this – as sometimes I did – I blanked the thought from my mind. I could not contemplate the fact that I, a well-balanced all-rounder, could actually be in the grip of an eating disorder. So I began to live a lie, a lie to others and a lie to myself.

The first signal that something might be physically wrong with me was when I realised that I had had no period in three months. This was in the summer of Lower 6th and I was doing exams. I did not go to the doctor because of the absent periods, but I had abdominal pain one Saturday and attended the out-of-hours service with my mum. She mentioned the periods because she was worried that there might be a gynaecological problem. I actually had lost little weight at this stage and the doctor did not consider dieting in his differential; instead, he diagnosed constipation and told me that my periods would probably come back during the holidays when stresses at school had passed. It didn't seem like an unreasonable explanation, but in fact a vital warning had been missed. I didn't have another period for over three years.

I remember that summer being relatively normal. I went on a trip to the Ukraine for three weeks to work with immigrant children, as well as on a family holiday, and I don't recall struggling particularly with eating; however, it was when I went back to school in September 1999 that people began to comment on my appearance. Initially, they did not tell me that I looked awful; just that I had lost enough weight and shouldn't lose any more. I was secretly flattered. I have a clear memory of looking at my bottom in my granny's bathroom mirror and feeling a sense of pride that I had managed to change it from what had always seemed to be an over-protuberant part of my anatomy to one that was neater and more pert. Later, I would look at its flaccid skin and bony angles with fear and horror.

I continued with my diet-disguised-as-healthy-eating, with my swimming sessions and now – increasingly – with excessive study. Others admired me for my conscientiousness; the truth was that I needed to fill my brain with academic knowledge to drown out the depressing thoughts and ominous feelings which were becoming more and more of a problem. By this stage, I had committed myself to studying medicine, although I had chosen to defer my entry by a year. I was also taking four A-levels, which was unusual at that time, so my rigorous work regimen was easy to justify. Occasionally, my parents or friends would tell me that I needed to chill out a bit more, but I would react angrily and they would back down. I would have liked to be able to 'chill', but I honestly didn't know how any more. Empty time frightened me.

By Christmas, I was unwell by any standard. I could not even relax my rules about food for Christmas dinner, watching over my mum's shoulder as usual to make sure my plate was loaded with vegetables and not meat, that all fat was trimmed off, and that no gravy was poured on the potatoes; I was continuing to over-exercise; and I insisted on reading textbooks whilst others enjoyed the festivities. Yet I managed to convince all around me that I was simply more disciplined than they were. Indeed, I realised later that some people were beginning to find me irksome and holier-than-thou. I lost friends because of it.

It should have rung alarm bells when I was able to buy lots of less-than-half-price clothes in the sales because I was one of only a few people who actually wore UK size

6. In the spring term, Upper 6th formers could wear their own clothes rather than uniform and I returned to classes with a whole new wardrobe of long skirts and elegant tops, with which I was rather pleased. I was not so pleased when they began to draw more attention to my figure, however. On one occasion, my neighbour in history class commented on how scary my exposed forearm looked; on another, I overheard a girl make a rude remark about my skinny legs. Still, I told myself that they were just jealous.

By Easter, my teachers were worried too. In French class, a fuss was made when I refused a Creme Egg and, although I didn't learn about this until later, the Vice Principal responsible for pastoral care phoned my mum to express concern and ask whether I was eating. My mum reassured her that I was eating plenty, that she knew I had lost weight, but the doctor had said I was just a bit stressed and would bounce back. This surprises me because, by this stage, I was beginning to fight with my parents over meals. Mum was getting offended when I wouldn't eat a fatty casserole, and irritated when I checked repeatedly that she wasn't putting any butter in the mash.

It seems that my parents took seriously my constant protestations that there was nothing wrong. After all, I had always been a very honest child, and they could see no reason that I would lie to them now. They have also told me since that it was hard for them to accept that I could have an eating disorder when I had always been such a happy person and, to all intents and purposes, seemed to be happy still.

I don't think I recognised myself at this stage just how unhappy I was. The lack of food was making me numb; the excessive exercise, euphoric; the constant studying, distracted. Unlike most depressed people, I was still goal-directed. I wanted my four Grade A's to get me into medical school, I was making plans for a gap year teaching English abroad, and I was applying for summer jobs to help me earn money to fund my travel. In fact, it was at the medical exam for one of these jobs, a few days after the end of my exams, that my weight was first flagged as a serious issue. My BMI was only 16, well below the healthy range of 18.5-25, and the occupational health physician was worried that I would be unfit for my busy hospital catering post. I told him what the other doctor had said over a year ago – that it was just exam-related stress – and that I was still fit and healthy otherwise. He accepted this and did not even refer me back to my own GP. I started the job a week later.

Working in the hospital suited me perfectly. I did some days in the shop, stacking shelves and operating the till; I took a trolley of papers and magazines on a long walk around the wards; and I worked other days in the canteen, slaving over a hot server or doing heavy vacuuming and cleaning. I was constantly on the move, always burning energy, and I had an excuse because I was getting paid for it. Even then, it wasn't enough for me: I had to be on the go all the time because of growing agitation. So, when colleagues were chatting over lunch, I was finishing my tiny packed one quickly and heading out for a walk in the grounds 'to clear my head'. When I had finished my shift, I would come home to walk the dog, 'because I needed some fresh air'. On rare days off, I deep-cleaned mum's house, 'because I enjoyed being useful'. There was always a plausible explanation, and, whilst others felt they couldn't keep up with me, no one seemed to think that I was mentally ill.

I did, all the same, begin a round of seeing doctors. My mum was worried because my period had not returned, and my GP sent me to a gynaecologist. The gynaecologist took my history, briefly examined me, and told me that he did not think I had a problem which he could help me with, but that he would refer me to an endocrinologist at the hospital where I was working. He did not tell me his presumed diagnosis; however, I learnt this at the endocrinology clinic, where I saw the registrar. She looked at the referral letter and wrote clearly at the top of the page, 'Anorexia Nervosa'. I began to protest. I knew I was cutting corners with my eating, but I was constantly justifying it to myself, telling myself I was only following well-known guidelines; I knew I was hyperactive, but I was justifying that too on the basis that only 15% of metabolised energy is due to exercise (most is used up in bodily processes).

The registrar weighed me and examined me and told me she was very concerned about how much I was eating. I insisted that there must be something else wrong with me if I was so sick, because I was eating just like the rest of my family. This actually became something of a swansong for me with successive doctors; however the truth was that, whilst I was eating with my family, I was carefully avoiding the fats my mum was now trying to add, skimping on the meals which I ate elsewhere, and exercising to such an extent that it was indeed using up far more energy than anyone could replace. The doctor opened up to me and said that she herself had had anorexia when she was a student, and that she could help me, but I had to try to eat more and she wanted me to gain a pound before she saw me in two weeks' time. When she said that, something clicked in my brain. I became determined to show that I was really ill – not inflicting this on myself – and I began for the first time to lose weight in a calculated manner.

Writing this, it seems warped that I would engage in such deceit, but the reality is that that is the power an eating disorder has. I knew I was unwell but could not accept that the problem was in my mind, so I convinced myself that there was a physical illness causing my weight loss and began to tell people this. Looking back, I'm sure it must have seemed odd that someone so physically ill had the energy to work as hard as I was working, always with a smile on my face, but I genuinely attracted a lot of sympathy. My parents were 100% behind me. Even though they continued to argue with me about the amount of exercise I was taking and my pickiness about food, they used to say that I shouldn't be like that because it would prove the doctors' point rather than because they too believed I was anorexic.

The situation became more and more complicated. I saw the consultant endocrinologist, who frightened me by carrying out an intimate and frankly abusive examination in front of my mum, whom I think he wanted to scare into doing something about my behaviour. He too declared me anorexic, at which point I decided I was not going back to his clinic. After this, an uncle who is a doctor - also deceived by my story that I knew I was eating more calories than I was expending yet still losing weight - recommended that I see a gastroenterologist whom he knew. He wrote a personal letter explaining my good character and that he found it hard to accept that I had an eating disorder, suggesting that I should instead be investigated for malabsorption. The gastroenterologist was kinder than the endocrinologist, and – whilst he later told me that he felt my story did not add up from the beginning – he agreed to do the relevant tests.

So it was that I submitted myself to an upper gastrointestinal endoscopy and a painful colonoscopy, not to mention endless blood tests, all of which were, naturally, negative. Even though I knew at one level that my eating was a problem, I needed to believe that it was not the only thing wrong. I felt that, if I started to eat more and began to look better, people would just assume I had had an eating disorder. On the contrary, if the doctors found something small wrong with my gut and could fix it, then I could start eating more, gain weight and put it all down to the physical problem rather than admitting to mental illness.

Perversely, I began to hope for news of some defect every time another test result came through. At the same time, I was still actively trying to lose weight so that I would still be seen to be ill. Sunday morning was my 'weigh day'. I would strip naked in the bathroom before my meagre breakfast and step onto the scales, praying that they would tip lower than the week before. Almost invariably they did, by about half a pound a time. Each week, my mum would simply say, 'Well?' I would shake my head, indicating that I had lost again. I would see her turn away in tears.

I was due to leave for Indonesia in January 2001, but a medical opinion was required in late October to approve me as fit to travel. I was still desperate to go, hoping that maybe I could miraculously recover whilst away and resume normal life when I got home, but the verdict was inevitable: the gastroenterologist could not pronounce me well enough whilst I was so underweight and losing with no known cause. Having exhausted his own options, he suggested that a friend of his, another endocrinologist at a different hospital, should see me for an opinion. He said that perhaps he could admit me to the metabolic ward and run some more tests, measuring my energy input and output very accurately. This probably should have scared me more as it would presumably have revealed that I was cheating, but I think I had begun to believe my own lie by this stage and was clutching at straws in any case. I was saddened that I couldn't travel but the alternative of being admitted to hospital would surely affirm to the world that I really was ill and not just failing to feed myself.

At the same time, I felt that I really needed to justify being put in hospital – something which was at that time alien to me – and the knowledge that I was to become an inpatient actually made me worse. I had had to stop working because of weakness but I began to exercise even more frantically to compensate, going for long cycle rides over hilly terrain and walking in severe weather conditions several times a day. I remember one occasion when my mum pulled up beside my bike as I struggled against wind and hail. I refused to get in, insisting that I needed to unwind with all the stress I was under. I also remember that I would practise my flute whilst on a step machine in my bedroom, burning calories whilst people just thought I was playing music. With hindsight, I think that I was perhaps almost manic at this time. I was certainly unusually restless and agitated, unable to sit or to sleep.

After a painful Christmas when I attempted to avoid eating in front of anyone and desperately tried to continue my exercise regimen in spite of my family's concerns, I was given a bed in hospital. I don't think I realised how desperately sick I was by this stage, though the few photos which remain from the time are hard to look at because I appear so gaunt and pale. I know that it can be triggering to other anorexics to read what weight people reach at their lowest, because they can feel like a failure if they are not as underweight, so I will not record the details. Suffice it to say that I was at a stage where heart or kidney failure could have set in at any moment.

For the first few days, I was given the benefit of the doubt, treated as a patient with an unknown physical illness. I had decided to eat normally, though I ordered the lightest menu options, and made sure people saw that I was clearing my plate. But some of my more bizarre habits were hard to hide. I could not relax for an instant, rocking back and forth on my bed as I feverishly completed jigsaw puzzles or cross-stitched; doing crosswords whilst standing up, and walking to the bathroom every half an hour. The nurses began to comment and, on day three, the consultant came to tell me that I was to be put on bed rest. I would have a commode brought to me if I needed the bathroom, and I would wash from a basin provided by a nurse. I was horrified, but I thought it was just to check I wasn't bulimic, which I wasn't, and that they would relax the rules after a few days. I was wrong. Searches were carried out to make sure I wasn't storing food or vomit, but an eating disorder, or 'nutrition problem', as my consultant called it, thinking I would find this easier to deal with, became the presumed diagnosis once more, and I was to remain on bed rest until I was healthier.

All the same, there were more tests, including a scan of my whole body after radioactive white blood cells had been injected to detect inflammation, contrast x-rays to outline areas of my bowel potentially missed by my endoscopies, an MRI scan to rule out a brain or pituitary tumour, and blood tests for rare conditions such as 'cat-scratch disease'. All were negative, and the attitude of staff changed towards me. It was not a psychiatric ward and there was little sympathy for the 'little anorexic girl', as the nurses called me. I even overheard them complain that I was wasting a bed, not to mention everyone's time. Naturally, I wanted more and more to go home.

But in order to be allowed to leave, I had to reach a 'target weight'. I was expected to gain half a pound a day, which is actually now considered to be a dangerous rate, risking 're-feeding syndrome'; however, once I stopped the relentless exercising, I did achieve this fairly steadily. Each morning at 6am, a nurse would wheel me to the scales, weigh me, and tell me 'Well done' in a patronising tone if I had gained. At the ward round, doctors would scarcely look at me, glancing instead at my weight chart, nodding approvingly, and moving on. Once, a registrar did stay to talk to me. She wanted to tell me that she knew a girl at medical school who had a 'problem like mine' and that she couldn't complete the course. Her point was that I shouldn't try to study medicine; if anything, she only strengthened my resolve.

An eating disorders specialist was brought to see me one day, spending an exhausting two hours asking me questions. Actually, she didn't draw any definite conclusions. I wasn't in any doubt that I was underweight, which is unusual in anorexics, who tend to have a grossly disturbed body image, and I was eating quite willingly at this stage. What seems odd is that there was no psychological follow-up arranged, but perhaps this was because I was so adamant that I neither wanted nor needed it.

My parents hated seeing me so miserable, bullied by nurses, unable to shower or stretch my legs, and labelled with a diagnosis which they still did not believe. My mum came up with a book which described a regime for people with bowel problems – specifically constipation, which was a genuine problem for me – and she suggested that, when I got home, I could try it. It was supposed to be composed of simple foods which needed less digestion, and, having read it, I felt that maybe it would be useful to me. It could help the constipation and also be an excuse for gaining weight as I could say that I was on a 'special diet' for people with malabsorption. This was to be my line for a long time to come; it was not until I relapsed several years later and went through family therapy that I told my parents how much I had hidden from them during this period.

Eventually, my consultant allowed them to take me home, a little way off my target but headed in the right direction. My discharge letter said 'weight loss, unknown aetiology', which I then thought was a euphemism for eating disorder but which I later learnt simply meant that the cause had not been determined. Despite the unkind treatment I had received whilst there, which was unjustifiable regardless of my own dishonesty, the nurses were thanked and I walked, tentatively on my wasted legs, from the ward. I had been an inpatient for almost five weeks, which seemed like an eternity at the time but which, compared to later psychiatric admissions, seems like quite a short while now.

At home, I did well. I stuck to the meal plan in the book my mum had come across, and drank the Fortijuce prescribed by my dietician. Despite not having any psychological input, I coped with the on-going weight gain, and the dark thoughts and feelings which I had been blunting with my anorexia seemed to have passed. The opportunity to go to Indonesia was no longer available, but I travelled instead to stay with family in the United States for a few weeks, and later to Eastern Europe, where I worked for a month in children's camps. This was a relief to me because it meant that, when I started medical school, I could say that I worked in a hospital and then abroad when people asked me what I did in my gap year. No one need know that I had had anorexia, a word which I still could not say.

I did go to medical school in September 2001 and, although my weight was still at the low end of normal, I remained healthy. I kept drinking Fortijuce at break times, which must have seemed odd to the other students, but if any of them asked about it, I simply said that I had been ill and needed to build myself up. My mood was good and I found that I enjoyed my studies but could approach them in a balanced manner, unlike the way in which I had tackled my A-levels. I took exercise every day but not to excess, enjoying salsa dancing with friends or Pilates classes rather than solitary activities like walking and cycling.

After two years of studying, I began to get more relaxed about my eating, breaking the rules of the special diet from time to time, until I decided to give it up altogether. It had clearly been helping me, because my constipation and irritable bowel returned, but being able to eat more freely helped my social life so much that I never contemplated returning to it. My GP eventually decided that I no longer required the extra calories from Fortijuce either, which was another step in the direction of normality.

And so it was that anorexia left my life for five years. When it returned, it was to be in a different form, much more obviously related to clinical depression, and this time formally diagnosed as 'EDNOS' or eating-disorder-not-otherwise-specified, but that is a story for another day...

Most people assume that anorexia stems from a traumatic childhood, from abusive or over-protective parenting. Indeed, many of my therapists have since tried to suggest to me that there must have been problems which I was blocking from my consciousness to avoid facing up to their reality. The truth could not be more different. I had what I would consider to be a fairly normal childhood. Certainly, my parents hit me from time to time when I was unruly, but no more than other parents whom I knew; and it never left me traumatised. On the whole, they were loving and supportive and I never doubted this even when their love was expressed in slightly odd ways.

We were a middle class family without a huge amount of spare money, but my parents tried to give my brother and sister and I every advantage which they could afford. I had swimming lessons, music lessons, riding lessons and a taxi service to youth groups and hockey practice. We holidayed fairly locally but always close to expansive beaches where we could gallop horses, swim and walk for miles, and mountains whose beauty always captivated me even though we were never particularly well equipped for hiking.

I was the eldest and probably set a difficult example for my brother to follow in terms of grades achieved and behaviour. Although close in age, we never shared a close relationship and today see each other infrequently; however, there is no animosity between us. My sister is much younger and has always been the most laid-back and outgoing of the family. Despite the age gap, we are close and still spend time together regularly.

There is no doubt that my anorexia had a huge effect on my family. Now when I see friends I have met through treatment but who have not recovered, I can understand how afraid and powerless they must have felt. It is incredibly difficult to watch someone you care about lose weight week by week, becoming so emaciated that you know there is a risk they will die. Because there was so much denial in my case – both on my part and on the part of my mum - things were even more complicated. Eventually we all came to deal with it in our own ways, and today that symptom of my developing mental illness is never spoken of, probably because it created the biggest strain on relationships.

Some say that no one ever fully recovers from an eating disorder; that at best they learn to manage it. After this first episode, I learnt to manage it, or perhaps did not need it. I really began to enjoy medical school from my third year, when I began clinical placements and had more contact with patients. I was an elected representative for my year and became a member of various faculty committees, making something of a name for myself as I campaigned for more formal teaching on the wards and regular changes to exam papers to prevent students with contacts in senior years gaining an unfair advantage. I also started to excel in most placements and won runner-up prizes in Medicine and Surgery, Paediatrics and Rheumatology.

Unfortunately, in my fourth year, things began to go wrong. In the first term, I developed a complication of an arthritic condition which I was suffering from at the time and needed surgery to remove a fistula which had formed in a bursa at my left Achilles tendon. I was in plaster to my knee and non-weight-bearing on crutches, but I was determined to carry on with clinical placements. This was a mistake. I became more and more exhausted and started having severe back pain which persisted even once I was walking again. My sleep became disturbed and my ability to concentrate was reduced. I was not depressed, but I was definitely tired. The crunch came during my obstetrics and gynaecology placement. I was expected to stay with four women throughout their labour and assist with their delivery. The problem was that I simply didn't have the stamina. Every labour that I attended went on for at least 12 hours, and I kept on needing to leave before the birth because I needed sleep so badly.

I failed to complete the course requirements and ended up in the office of the Senior Tutor, who was thankfully more concerned about what was happening from a pastoral perspective than from a disciplinary one. I explained that I had seen deliveries on work experience previously and eventually it was agreed that – as long as I could pass the written and clinical exams - I would not need to repeat the placement.

It was a good outcome, but it started a process in my head which ultimately led to a decision to take another year out before fifth year. Together with two friends who had also recovered from eating disorders, I had been running a support service for students with eating disorders for most of my undergraduate career. At that time, it consisted of a drop-in centre in a chaplaincy building on Wednesday afternoons (which were free of classes so that students could participate in extra-curricular activities) and an email helpline, but demand was growing and the chaplains were keen to keep it going. I didn't think any of us would have time to maintain it during our final year, so I met with one of the chaplains and mooted the idea that I could take on the role full-time for one year whilst they found a way to make the service sustainable. There was already a volunteer programme in place and the plan would be that I would join this; however, I would need approval from the faculty first. The chaplains were excited by the idea and encouraged me to pursue it. I was surprised that the Dean of the medical school approved it without even asking to meet me, and so things began to fall into place.

I finished fourth year and then, rather than prepare for my final year, I joined the chaplaincy team as leader of the eating disorder project. I was given a serviced office, funding for literature and the promise of supervision and pastoral support. The chaplaincy also offered to pay for a counselling course which would help me to develop the skills I needed for the task ahead. I made plans for a number of services. There was now to be a telephone helpline as well as the email facility; I would offer support with a self-help cognitive behavioural therapy programme for people with bulimia; students would be able to make appointments for 'peer support'; and I would run a programme of training seminars and awareness-raising events throughout the year.

For the first few months, the service could not have been better received. By Christmas, over 60 students had been in touch. Most were directed to appropriate help; some became regulars at the chaplaincy, coming for a chat or sometimes simply to cry in a supportive environment. The university staff, local youth leaders and students who attended seminars all gave excellent feedback, and plans for the February awareness week were well under way, with five student volunteers assisting me.

However, in January, things began to go wrong. I was called to a meeting with the funding board and told that there would not be money from the chaplaincy to pay for a replacement support officer the following year; instead, it was going to suicide prevention. I was desolate. There was no way that I could continue in the role as I was still committed to medicine and wanted to finish my degree. Frantically, I began seeking out alternative ways to keep the service going. I looked into the possibility of setting it up as an independent charity, trying to find people willing to be trustees, but without success. I met with several counsellors who had expressed interest in being involved longer term, but when they realised the scale of the operation and the numbers of students for whom they would have a certain responsibility, each of them decided the role was not tenable.

All the while, I continued to work hard, unwilling to let the students know that anything was amiss. The awareness week reached literally thousands as a short film which we made about a bulimic student was featured on the regional news and shown in a local cinema, later winning a national award for its screenplay. A service was held for sufferers and their families and friends, an evening celebrating the art of sufferers was well attended, and I spoke at a number of student societies. At the same time, I could feel myself burning out. What could I do to make sure all of my work was not in vain? I had an idea. I would make a website with links to every source of help I had been directing students to; all of the training resources which I had developed and articles which I had written; and as much information about eating disorders in students as I could find.

Thankfully, I had a friend who could help me. Together, we developed an impressive site which was secure and user-friendly; however, when I told the chaplains and a representative of the local NHS eating service about it, they insisted that it could not go online. There was too much risk involved, they said. What if students who read it became more ill? I would be responsible. What if it was abused and people wrote pro-anorexia comments on it? I insisted that it could only be modified by the site manager. No matter how staunchly I argued, they were insistent. I went home to see my parents in floods of unstoppable tears.

From this point on, I felt unsupported. I was not getting enough supervision to help me deal with the emotional problems students were presenting with, I could not find a way to ensure that the service did not collapse at the end of my term, and I felt as if I would have no legacy. I held out hope until May, and then realised that I was going to have to tell my students the truth. As of

September, their peer support and advice service would be gone. It was heartbreaking. So many asked if I would keep in touch personally. I had to say no. Some reminded me of my assurances that there would be a replacement when I was gone. I felt like a fraud. The worst was that I kept bumping into them around the university and they would simply look down, unsure whether they were even allowed to speak to me any more. I wasn't sure myself.

I wound the service up in June. It was around this time that I had a 'breakdown'. Within weeks I was diagnosed with depression, the subject of my next chapter. As time went on, the symptoms (or phenomena) described in subsequent chapters developed, and ultimately I was diagnosed with schizoaffective disorder. Who knows? Perhaps that could change with time too. Mental illness is hard to define: I am diagnosis in evolution.

Chapter 3

Depression

Imagine looking at the most vivid image you can think of – a springtime flower garden, an impressionist painting – and seeing it in monochrome, drained of colour. Imagine listening to your favourite piece of music – a powerful rock ballad, Rachmaninov – and hearing it tuneless, off-key. Imagine eating your favourite food and being unable to taste anything, smelling your favourite perfume and feeling nauseated, stroking your favourite material and recoiling in disgust. It seems that every one of your senses is compromised, tainted by something you cannot name.

Imagine that you love to read but suddenly you cannot concentrate; you find yourself reading and re-reading the same page and being unable to follow the narrative. Imagine that you love to write creatively but suddenly you find yourself staring at a blank screen, unable to find words. Imagine that you enjoy socialising but suddenly you hate being in company, avoiding occasions when you might be expected to engage in conversation, to smile and to make eye contact. Imagine that you have a beloved dog whose affectionate attempts to win your attention suddenly go ignored. Imagine that you have a job or do a course which stimulates and challenges you, and suddenly you drag yourself there in the morning only to feel like you just want to go straight back home. Imagine that you enjoy taking exercise but suddenly you find it too much effort, capable only of lying on the sofa instead.

The air around you feels heavy and oppressive. You feel as if you are swimming underwater, your perception of the world around you distorted by its ripples and waves. Your thinking is clouded and slowed, the cogs of your brain sticking together, needing oiled. People speak to you and you stare blankly back at them, failing to register what they have said. You are living in an altered world.

In bed at night, negativity flows through your consciousness, but sleep refuses to set you free. "I'm useless. I'm a failure. What have I done wrong to feel like this? Things are never going to be better..." When, finally, you do drift off, it is into a world of nightmares. You dream about your own funeral, the coffin on a stand, blood dripping from it as mourners look on, aghast. In your semi-sleep, you hear witches cackle at you, demons mocking you. You shudder, suddenly wide awake. You realise it is 2.30am, yet you know that you will lie there until morning, tossing, turning, tormented.

Caring for yourself becomes a trial. You have no appetite, nor the energy to cook. You live on cereal, on biscuits, the occasional meal of beans-on-toast. All of it has the texture of cardboard. Gradually, weight drops from your body. You see a gaunt face staring back at you from the mirror, and people begin to ask if you are unwell. But it seems pointless to make more of an effort. You continue to wash, to shower, though the water falls harshly on your skin, but getting dressed is more difficult. Your wardrobe is full of pretty colours and delicate fabrics, but all you want to wear is black. The colours do not fit your feelings, you do not want to be noticed.

As time goes by without improvement, you begin to have what psychiatrists call 'TLNWL' – thoughts that life is not worth living. It is not so much that you think life in general is pointless; it seems OK for other people. It is just your life which is too starved of joy and filled with tribulation; it is you who feels too exhausted to persevere any further. Dark day follows dark day, troubled night follows troubled night, and you wonder whether you can really carry on. Life – this treadmill you are walking – does indeed seem pointless. At first, these thoughts are fleeting; as time goes by, you begin to dwell on them more and more. As you dwell on them, you may start to tentatively think about alternatives to carrying on, very vaguely to begin with, then forming tentative plans or hypothetical scenarios. Somehow, these are not frightening so much as comforting. The thought that you have the option of dying if and when you need to actually gives you the strength to keep living, for a time at least.

This, to me, is depression.

At times, my depression has manifested itself in a profoundly physical way. When I am depressed, I am overwhelmed by fatigue. I can remember periods at the beginning of my illness when I would drag myself out of bed in the morning and walk to the nearby hospital for my placement. I would arrive so exhausted that I would slip out of the ward round and go to the canteen for a cup of coffee to revive me before the clinic or theatre time. I would feel better for five or ten minutes, but then fade again on my way to wherever I was expected, turning instead towards home. Often I would find myself back in my student accommodation before 9.30am, collapsing in a heap on my bed and wondering what on earth was wrong with me.

On other days, I would be timetabled for lectures from 9am-5pm. All that was required of me was to sit and listen, but I would feel so tired that I could not concentrate beyond the first hour. Usually I would find myself in the canteen again, then back at home printing hand-outs for the rest of the day from the Internet and scanning them quickly for key facts so that I didn't need to be there in person.

For weeks at a time, I would be unable to sleep. Lack of sleep can cause fibromyalgia – pain in the muscles – and this led to a vicious cycle for me. My back muscles would become tight and go into spasms, which would keep me awake, leading to more muscle pain, and so on. I became so stiff and sore that, when I was referred to a physiotherapist, all she could do to begin with was take me to the warm hydrotherapy pool to soothe my pain; any hands on mobilisation of joints or exercise programme was impossible. With time, I loosened up a little, but back pain remains a harbinger of depression for me to this day, although now I can take sleep medication to break the cycle of insomnia sooner and I do yoga to help keep me flexible.

As well as back pain, I suffered from horrendous migraines. At one stage they began to come every day and 'cluster headaches' were diagnosed, although technically this term refers to headaches of shorter duration than the ones I experienced. These came at times of stress, but it was a long time before I made a connection between mental health problems and the very physical symptoms I was having.

For me, though, the most visible sign of my depression was definitely weight loss. As I have previously written about, I had suffered from anorexia long before I was diagnosed with depression. This had certainly been associated with low mood and strange thoughts, but had also demonstrated a fairly clear picture of anorexia nervosa, that is, inadequate nutritional intake due to fear of weight gain. I had made a full recovery from this, yet in August 2006, when clinical depression was diagnosed, I began to lose weight again very rapidly.

This time around, I was not thinking about my body or worrying about becoming fat, and I was not calculatedly losing weight; however, I found it very difficult to eat properly for all kinds of reasons. I had genuinely lost my appetite, which is a symptom of depression for most people, and I was also aware of a tightness in my stomach which made it physically difficult to swallow a large meal. With such a low mood, I lacked any motivation to cook for myself properly, and I shunned meals with others because I had no desire or mental energy to be sociable. In contrast to my teenage anorexia, I had no particular rules around food or items which I had to avoid, so if I was at the hospital and working on into the evening, I would often eat a chocolate cookie and drink a cappuccino to keep me going, and then fail to have dinner later on. I bought microwave meals for when I was at home, tending to choose those with smaller portions because the sight of a big plate of food would put me off eating altogether.

Some of the effects of my low calorie intake were the same as before, however I started to become numb to the dark feelings, and my thoughts were somehow clearer. I started to exercise more too, not deliberately, but because of the ways in which I was coping with my low mood. For example, I was on placement in a hospital which was a twenty minute walk away from home during the first half of my final year, when my first official diagnosis was made. Because I couldn't cope with long stretches of time on the wards, and couldn't bear to socialise with other students over lunch, I walked back and forth to the solace of my own space several times a day. I found that the fresh air and rhythm of walking boosted my sense of well-being, and the journey became a sort of ritual.

I reached a point where I was living in a kind of paradox of utter exhaustion and nervous, agitated energy. Since

I was getting no enjoyment from any of my usual interests in life – a state known as anhedonia – I threw all of this nervous energy into my final year course. Being in the hospital as much as possible kept my mind and body occupied and saved me from thinking about how I really felt. I knew that looking my thoughts square in the face would terrify me; occupying myself with other people's ailments served as a distraction therapy. But of course all of my frantic midnight assessments of admission patients and early morning presentations at ward rounds expended energy. I became thinner and thinner.

It was not long before people began to comment, to ask me if I was well. I knew that I was not but laughed off my appearance, saying I'd been working a bit too hard but that I was fine. I knew that to tell the truth would lead to a breakdown; I could not allow reality to bite. Still, I could not hide the problem from my psychiatrist, a registrar to whom I had been referred on an urgent basis when I first presented to my GP with thoughts that my life wasn't worth living. He noted that I looked gaunt at my first appointment, weighed me and realised that my BMI was already significantly below the recommended minimum. Having questioned me about body image and recognised that my mood was the primary problem, he diagnosed 'moderate to severe depression with eating disorder not otherwise specified'. The latter term, often shortened to 'EDNOS', is commonly used when the full complement of diagnostic criteria for anorexia or bulimia are not met. From then on, he would weigh me at each visit; at each visit, I had invariably lost.

I was taking antidepressants at this time but they were not helping, and each new one added had side effects which limited the dose. My frenetic energy reached a peak at which I was considered a model student by all of the hospital doctors because I was always around - doing an ECG here, taking bloods there - and then rapidly declined. I had reached a critical point as far as my weight was concerned and it was becoming difficult to retain an upright posture on the over-stuffy wards, whilst mentally I was no longer able to think clearly and instead was zoning out, staring blankly when asked a question, trailing off half way through my own sentences. December 2006 was the last month which I was to spend on placement.

My experience of depression is unusual because there are so many contradictions in my history. I was first admitted to hospital in January 2007 because of my physical frailty and the content of my thoughts, which often strayed to suicide, and was sectioned three weeks later when I wanted to leave; yet I continued to study each day in the ward, determined that, if I was going to live, I would pass my finals. These days, when I become depressed, I scarcely have the drive to wash and dress myself. My goals have gone, my dreams have passed me by; back then, I think I was still working towards a Plan B. If this gets better I'll be a doctor and I'll understand how patients with mental illness feel, I said to myself. I still thought that a psychiatric hospital must be a positive place, one where people were helped towards healing, rather than merely a place of safety. I know now that there are in existence institutions where therapy is the core, but the ward where I was kept in custody at that time was not one of them.

In hospital my condition deteriorated. I remember long, sleepless nights, punctuated only by short, restless nightmares. I remember crying so hard and for so long that a nurse told me that, if I had been a sponge, she would have picked me up and wrung me out. People would visit me and I would first cry and then stare through them, unable to muster up a conversation. I could not grasp the pitifulness of my state, kept as a ward of the court against my will in a place where people talked to invisible beings or compared stories of suicide attempts. And yet, whilst I could not go on placements, I left the ward twice weekly for evening tutorials with fellow students who did not officially know I was unwell (although I later learnt that most of them had worked it out), and continued to make little themed cards with key learning points for each condition – cards which I still have to this day.

My capacity to study lessened, however, and the day of my clinical exams was not a good one. The irony of the situation – leaving the psychiatric ward where I was a patient to don my white coat and stethoscope for an exam which would make me a doctor in name only, since I knew by then that I would not be working – was not lost on me. I didn't know why I was putting myself through it, except that I had to, for my own sanity, even though I was contemplating later suicide.

I blanked in the first station, where I was to examine a patient with a heart murmur. Somehow, I couldn't remember the differences between examining the heart and examining the lungs. I mixed up my routines and, in my confusion, forgot to listen as I was placing my stethoscope in each position. When the assessor asked me to describe the abnormality, I told him the classical features of the commonest murmur. It turned out that my best guess had been wrong. The rest of the morning is a hazy memory, although the look of concern on the face of one assessor who had known me before I got sick will never leave me. I must have managed not to miss anything particularly significant, however, because I learnt a few days later that I had passed. My mum sent a big congratulatory bouquet with balloons attached to the ward. I burst every one and put the flowers in the bin. I could not see the point in congratulations. I had a degree, but I had no life. I was still depressed, still sectioned, still battling thoughts of suicide.

Depression then turned to emotional instability. This seems to have been due to the side effects of a particular drug which I was taking. I could be incredibly low but then recover suddenly, only to plunge into despair again. It was wearing, I was agitated, and my behaviour became chaotic. Not making the connection between the medication and my changed mental state, my then psychiatrist changed my diagnosis to borderline personality disorder, and my treatment plan was changed to involve treatment for my eating problems and for my dysfunctional coping strategies. It took two years of suffering and inappropriate interventions before anyone realised what was happening to me, but I have written of that elsewhere. Once I stopped the drug, my mood pattern became more typical of bipolar disorder, with sustained depressions and periods of elation as well.

I continue to suffer from depression to this day. In fact, I am battling through a mild episode as I write. Often, when my depression is not utterly debilitating, it seems to fuel the creative process; at other times, it extinguishes it completely.

I cannot take a job because of my depression. I do work some days, and in a fairly demanding role, but it has to be on a voluntary basis because of the amount of time which I need to take off and the limitations to my energy. For example, this morning, I went to work intending to spend a full day there, but I had to leave at lunchtime, needing a full two hours of rest before I could begin even to consider what I might do next. Fatigue is a major frustration for me, and it is not helped by my struggle to sleep. At the moment, my sleep is so disrupted that I get up in the morning feeling drained before the day begins. I have had desperate moments over the past week, calling a suicide helpline and visiting the out-of-hours GP, but I am managing to take things hour by hour, trying not to let the hopeless thoughts – the 'I'm never going to have a career, or a relationship, or children, so what's the point in going on?' thoughts – take hold of me completely.

Depression is a constant battle. For me, it is now punctuated with periods of hypomania and psychosis which complicate things further, but it is the depression which I dread most. It has been called the 'black dog'; for me, it is much more ominous – not something which follows me but something which subsumes me. I become it and it becomes me, something dark and limp and lifeless. That I still have life in spite of it is something of a miracle, though I don't always see it in such positive terms. At other times, I think that life free from depression would be less rich, because in depression one truly feels, in a deep, guttural way, the emotions which make one fully human. And one can appreciate the joys of the better times in glorious colour.

Depression is a constant battle, but one which, in some ways, I would not be without.

Chapter 4

Self-harm

Being a self-harmer is not fun. Being a self-harmer with a medical degree is probably less fun, though I can't say with absolute certainty because I haven't experienced it without one.

People tend to judge you for it, which is largely because they fail to understand it. This makes sense to me now that I am a non-self-harmer. The thought of putting a blade to my own skin and applying enough pressure to break it is unthinkable, utterly alien. We human beings have strong instincts to protect ourselves from harm, not to inflict it upon ourselves.

Yet what I yearned for more than anything in the two years that I was self-harming was for someone – anyone – to understand. Granted, some tried. They read leaflets which said that people self-harm for all kinds of reasons: to show in a tangible way that they are hurting inside, to release tension, because the physical pain distracts from the emotional pain for a time. But none of these reasons particularly struck a chord with me.

Most people who self-harm are given the diagnosis of emotionally unstable (or 'borderline') personality disorder, which is not considered to be an illness but a defect in the personality itself, which can sometimes be managed but never cured. This label often brings with it stigma. Personality-disordered people are thought to be difficult, attention-seeking, and self-centred, and there remains a lot of prejudice against them within the medical profession and even psychiatry. I remember a charismatic and – I thought – empathetic physician telling me whilst I was on attachment to his ward, "Don't even go near Mrs X. That woman has a personality disorder!"

In busy emergency departments, where self-harmers tend to present repeatedly, they are often considered to be wasting doctors' precious time. I lost count of how many times I was told I had to wait again because 'somebody who is actually sick' needed attention. At this stage, I too had a diagnosis of personality disorder.

I can remember clearly when I first had thoughts of hurting myself. For me, it happened in the week that I was started on a new antidepressant, Effexor (also known by its generic name, venlafaxine). What I didn't know at the time, and was not told, was that this drug came with a warning to prescribers advising them to be alert for changes in the patient's mental state because there was a risk of self-harm and suicidal ideation, especially in people aged less than 25. I was 24 years old. My parents were frightened by what I was telling them about my thoughts, and asked to speak with my psychiatrist, even wanting to take me home from hospital. He listened but responded that they had to leave my treatment to him; I was now a ward of the court, held under a detention order, and they had no longer any influence over me.

Being in hospital, I had little opportunity to act on my thoughts at the time, although I made a few attempts to scratch myself; it was later, when I was an outpatient, that things got out of control. Perhaps that is why no one was alerted to the paradigm shift which I knew had occurred inside my brain.

I still recall the first occasion that I used a razor blade. I was living in rented accommodation and my student housemates had not moved in for the autumn semester yet. I was feeling incredibly agitated and tried to start watching The West Wing (which later became my favourite TV series) but could not settle or concentrate. The thoughts of self-harm were intense. Almost frenzied, I took a plastic razor from the bathroom and slashed twice at my left forearm. I had not removed the blade (a trick I learnt later), so the cuts were not deep, but they bled freely. I panicked. This had to mean there was something seriously wrong with me. I wrapped my arm in tissue paper and ran, crying, to the door of the psychiatric ward I had left just weeks earlier. A nurse answered the doorbell but would not let me in. "You're not a patient here any more," she said; "If you need help, go to A&E." Dejected, I walked slowly home. I knew that my cuts would heal and I was too ashamed to go to an emergency department with self-harm knowing that my own former classmates would be working there. Little did I know how my embarrassment would end up becoming the last of my considerations as time went on.

I did end up back in hospital, still taking Effexor, and there my self-harming behaviour only increased, my agitation intensified by the contained and suffocating ward environment. Razors were not accessible, so my methods became more innovative. I would stealthily slip a plastic teaspoon up my sleeve during a meal, and later snap it in half when I was alone, using the jagged edge to scrape my skin; or I would wait until the supervising nursing auxiliary was looking away and pour scalding water over my arm at tea-time. Eventually, I ended up under 'close observation' at all times, assigned a personal nurse to watch over me. On one dreadful occasion, I persuaded my nurse to let me shave my now-hairy legs in the bath, genuinely believing that I would be safe and convincing her of this too. Unfortunately, she trusted me to do it without her watching face-on, the urge overtook me and I sliced into my skin. The nurse almost cried. She had trusted me and now she could not forgive herself. I cried too, devastated to have abused her trust and potentially damaged her career.

I still did not know why I was self-harming. My psychiatrist thought he knew. My behaviour had become chaotic, he said, and I no longer showed evidence of pervasive low mood as I had done on my previous admission. He said that I had a 'complex set of problems' and told my parents that I had a personality disorder and not major depressive disorder as had previously been diagnosed. Plans were even made to send me to a specialist unit in London for treatment of Severe Personality Disorder, a thought which terrified me. I could not be forced to go there, however, because they did not take sectioned patients, and I reneged on the offer.

The worst of my self-harm occurred after I returned from six months of eating disorder treatment in America. I was still taking the maximum dose of Effexor, still incredibly agitated, and feeling by this stage as if I was a hopeless case because I had had more interventions than any other patient I knew yet was still feeling more desperate than ever for someone to help me first to understand what I was doing and second to actually stop it.

The first time that I required stitches the A&E doctor was relatively sympathetic, apparently sensing how traumatised I felt and how ashamed I was. "You haven't been here before with this, have you?" he asked. I said that this was correct. "And you regret what happened?" I nodded. What I didn't tell him was that I had, in fact, been trying to slit my wrists but that, somehow entirely forgetting the anatomy of the forearm, had made the cut on the upper aspect, where there are no arteries. I went home without a psychiatric assessment.

This episode proved to be a watershed. Once I had breached the skin to a depth where it needed to be sewn back together, I would never again feel that I had gone far enough unless I saw fatty tissue, muscle or blood vessels. Was I trying to punish myself? Was I seeking attention? I was certainly crying out for help. What I do not identify with is the idea that the pain of self-harm clouds emotional pain, for I rarely felt any pain when I was cutting myself. Perhaps in another sense, however, the act itself did work in this way, because once I had decided to cut, wherever I was, my entire focus became centred on finding something to do it with and getting myself to somewhere private. Sometimes I bought a blade in a chemist and cut myself in the unhygienic setting of a public toilet; sometimes I was at home and, in the absence of a razor blade (I often threw any I had out in an effort to break the cycle), cut myself with the lid of a tin can.

My life became a blur of A&E visits and tearful appointments with my GP, who was enormously supportive, especially given that I had, ostensibly, a personality disorder for which I had refused specialist treatment. At first, I found it incredibly difficult to present myself for treatment, knowing that my injuries were self-inflicted and that the doctors working there were - especially given the time lapse since I graduated - likely to be from my year group; as time went on, I became more numb, knowing the routine, avoiding eye contact, saying as little as possible.

Even though I began to rotate the hospitals which I visited, frequenting four in all, the staff in each got to know me. I would see nurses rolling their eyes when they saw me coming; the odd kinder one calling over,

"Has no one got you any help, yet, love?" Reception staff started to simply ask, "Same as usual?" whilst some triage assistants stopped bothering to check my vital signs, the possibility that I could have lost a significant amount of blood apparently lost on them.

Mostly, I waited for hours for my six or seven stitches, sometimes under the watchful eye of a nurse within the department in case I left, more usually in a cold and uncomfortable waiting room. The doctor would call me, suture me and discharge me, usually without offering a psychiatric assessment. Sometimes I refused the local anaesthetic. I felt guilty about taking it when I had made the cut in the first place, and also figured that if I wasn't sore already, a few stitches wouldn't cause pain either.

It was indeed often the case that the doctor knew me from my time at medical school, but rarely did they acknowledge this. The majority of them avoided conversation beyond asking me if I had any other injuries or if I was allergic to Elastoplast. I felt shunned, no longer a person to my former colleagues; instead, a self-harmer who should really know better. And there were some particularly bad experiences too. One girl who graduated in my class came into my cubicle without closing the curtain behind her, exposed my cut thigh, looked at it without speaking to me, left again, came back with a staple gun and fired 6 staples into my skin without even washing the wound. I looked at her and she just said, "You can go now." Inevitably, within a few days, the surrounding tissue was horribly infected. I required two further A&E visits for sepsis, three courses of antibiotics and re-closure of the wound before it finally healed. The scar is the widest I have today.

At one hospital, the policy was different, and patients who had self-harmed were held until a psychiatric nurse could assess them; however, for me this was a pointless exercise – although this hospital was nearby, it was outside the catchment boundary for my local mental health trust, so the nurse would inevitably discharge me and tell me to 'go to the right hospital' next time. Often I deliberately went there anyway if it was evening, knowing that at least they would keep me safe until daylight. The general policy in many Health Trusts is not to admit self-harmers to hospital in any case as it is not felt to be helpful, except occasionally for a three day 'respite'; after all, they are usually not considered to be mentally ill.

This laisser-faire policy almost led to my death however, as on two occasions I severed arteries and had severe bleeding. The first time, I simply cut deeper than I expected, just over the radial artery. Blood began to spurt everywhere, staining my sofa and splashing over the floor. I was utterly terrified and immediately called for an ambulance, trying desperately to mop up the pools of warm, red liquid as I made my way towards the door. I did not want my mum to find a bloodbath, and I wanted the ambulance to meet me on the road, away from my flat, so that my neighbours would not know what had happened. On that evening, the paramedics controlled the bleeding with a pressure bandage and, oddly, the A&E staff didn't even need to stitch me as the wound closed over itself during the night.

The second incident was much more dangerous. I had made a deep cut in my mid forearm when I suddenly thought that I just couldn't live this chaotic life any more. There was no quality to my existence; it had just become a merry-go-round of hospitals and drugs and distress. Impulsively, I grabbed a pair of scissors and snipped right through the radial artery. Blood sprayed my kitchen ceiling, walls, work surfaces and floor. I could feel myself becoming faint. Again, I had a terrible vision of my mum – the only other key-holder – walking into my flat to find my lifeless body lying on the ground in a scene from a horror movie. I couldn't bear to think of her going through that, of how she would relive the moment for the rest of her days. I tried to call an ambulance but the touchscreen of my phone was too wet to respond. Somehow, I managed to tourniquet my arm and stem the flow just enough so that I could wipe the screen and, increasingly weak, call 999.

"I've slit my wrist," I cried; "There's blood everywhere. I can't stop it." The operative told me the ambulance was on its way and that I shouldn't have tourniqueted my wrist. She assumed the bleeding was venous. I knew better and left it in place, staggering out to the road with blood pouring down my arm. I heard the siren almost immediately and soon the paramedics had my arm elevated and a pressure bandage over another pressure bandage. The police arrived at the same time and wanted to question me but I heard the ambulance driver say that there was no time – I had to get to A&E now. I learnt later that they had broken into my flat, so the neighbours did find out. Apparently this is routine as suicide is a crime. They also needed to check that the wounds were self-inflicted and no one else was around.

In the ambulance, I was sure I was going to die. The blue lights were flashing and the siren wailing. I was conscious but had to prove it to myself by keeping on talking to the paramedic, who was reassuring. In A&E they wheeled me straight to the resuscitation bay. I learnt later that I had lost 4 units of blood, yet still they sent me home late the same night without even asking me whether I still felt suicidal. I cleaned up my own flat with a large bandage covering my sutures before I even told my parents what had happened. In fact, I have never told them the full details of what happened that afternoon.

Sometime in the midst of this 5-month nightmare, I was referred to the local Self Harm Team. Once assessed, I was referred to a group, where people talked about their self-harm and, supposedly, worked on ways to stop the chain of events before the behaviour occurred. For me, there wasn't really a chain of events; everything happened so quickly from first thought to action. What's more, hearing other people describe their self-harm, often graphically, triggered the thoughts inside my own head. I don't think there was a single week during the two months that I attended when I did not go straight home and hurt myself. The groups were not helpful to me; in fact, it was clear that they were making me worse. I had a Self Harm Consultant Psychiatrist by this stage and she agreed with me, deciding to take me as an individual patient instead. The individual sessions did not help me but at least they did not aggravate the problem to the same extent.

Finally, I was admitted to a psychiatric hospital after a serious overdose in early summer 2009. There, things did not improve, but one day I had a kind of epiphany. The drugs I was taking were clearly not helping me, because I didn't see how there was any way that I could feel worse, and they might even be adding to my agitation. On Friday 2nd August, I started to refuse my medication – including the Effexor - at the trolley when my name was called. The nurses were aggrieved but could not force me to take it. My consultant was on holiday and the trainee was unavailable over the weekend. By the Tuesday ward round, I felt like a new person. A little jittery from withdrawal, but my mind was clearer and, most importantly, I had no thoughts of self-harm or suicide. The trainee couldn't deny the improvement in my mental state and did not try too hard to persuade me to start taking my medication again, although I agreed to take a low dose of a couple of my drugs so the tremor and sweats would be better controlled.

Over two years later, I can say that I still have no thoughts of harming myself. I cut once in February 2010, during a particularly bad episode of depression, really just to see if it did anything for me. It did not, I regretted it immediately, and I have never cut since. Hopefully, I never will again.

Chapter 5

Overdosing

Imagine that your head is spinning. Pain shoots through every nerve in your body. You are heaving bile into a kidney dish, surrounded by six or seven others already full of green vomit. When you breathe, you smell chemicals. You taste chemicals too. You are vaguely conscious of the lights and sounds around you, but they fade in and out. Yet you have only been given a chair to sit on, not a trolley or bed, and no one will give you anything for the pain or the sickness.

You have overdosed on Paracetamol, and you are at the bottom of the heap in A&E. Every department sees this happen every day. Most people who overdose are not considered to be mentally ill. In many cases they are seen to be a nuisance. What will happen to you is that blood samples will be taken 4 hours after you reported ingesting the drug, and – if the level of milligrams per millilitre of blood exceeds a certain threshold – you will receive an antidote, usually Parvolex. You may then feel worse, but no other medication can be given to you. Your liver is processing enough already. Its function will be monitored. If you are lucky, the enzymes produced when it is damaged will gradually fall; if you are not, a transplant may be considered, or you may die of liver failure. Survivors will have a pounding withdrawal headache which may last days.

Paracetamol overdose was glossed over in medical school, under the heading of 'Treatment of Acute Poisoning'. After all, from the medic's perspective, its treatment is straightforward. I was taught the treatment curve and how the threshold for antidote prescription was lower if the patient was malnourished or alcoholic. I was taught to conduct a quick assessment of suicide risk, but the A&E doctors who facilitated my placement rarely did one, referring patients directly to the on-call psychiatric nurse instead. No one ever taught me that these patients were really ill, that they felt as sick if not sicker than those in the beds around them with more palatable conditions. I only learnt that through hard experience.

The first time that I took an overdose the amount was so small that, in light of later events, it seems almost laughable that I even went to A&E. I was feeling incredibly depressed and agitated one evening in September 2007 and I went to my medication cupboard and found that I had six paracetamol tablets. I swallowed all of them – three times as many as should be taken in a single dose. About an hour later, I panicked. I felt a little unwell and wondered if my liver was failing. (Clearly, I had not understood pharmacology or physiology particularly well.) I was living just a few minutes' walk from the hospital, and I presented myself to the emergency department. There, I saw two of my former classmates at work. They looked over at me and I turned my eyes to the floor. When I was called to triage, I told the nurse what I had taken but that I wasn't sure after all whether it was significant and wondered if she could ask a doctor so that I could go home. She agreed and I saw her ask one of the girls from my class, who looked over again, her expression surprised this time. The nurse came back. "You've taken less than the full daily dose. If you aren't going to take any more, and you're getting psychiatric help, you can go home." I nodded in affirmation and left.

The next day, I got a phone call from a blocked number. It turned out to be an A&E consultant who had seen my notes from the night before and noticed that my occupation had been listed as 'doctor'. She wanted to know that I wasn't working and that I had sought help. I told her I was a day hospital patient and hadn't worked since graduation. It was kind of her to call, and good medical practice too, but I never again gave my occupation as doctor. I didn't want to be chased up. From that point on, I was 'unemployed'.

There is no such thing as an insignificant overdose, but the first time I took one serious enough to require treatment was only a few weeks later. I think that I had broken a taboo. They say that someone who has diced with death through a suicide attempt, no matter how half-hearted, is much likelier to complete suicide. They have mentally allowed themselves that little bit closer to crossing the great divide between life and death, which makes it easier for them to go the whole way from that point on.

I was absolutely desperate at this point in my life. My career had been taken from me, I was highly agitated – probably in part due to my antidepressant medication, and I could see no way out. I don't remember the exact circumstances of the act itself, but I will never forget the aftermath. In A&E, I was assessed by a girl with whom I had once been fairly friendly at medical school. She was actually really kind to me, sitting down on the bed at my level and saying how sorry she was to see me in this state. Her eyes told me she was genuine and her gentle touch was entirely non-judgemental. I had only taken 13 tablets, but my blood Paracetamol levels were high and I would need treatment, she told me. I was admitted under the medical team.

Once I had a bed, a Parvolex drip was begun. Parvolex is n-acetylcysteine, the best antidote to Paracetamol. If I felt unwell before the drip started, I soon began to feel much worse. I was dragging my drip pole to the toilet constantly because I was vomiting and had diarrhoea, but I assumed that this was just due to the poisoning. Soon I began to cough as well, and then to wheeze, and eventually a nurse came over to see me. She called for a doctor, who noticed a blotchy, swollen, red rash over my trunk and arms. Immediately, she stopped the Parvolex and called for her senior. I was having a severe allergic reaction. They gave me IV antihistamines and steroids, and soon I began to feel better. A decision was taken not to treat me with a different antidote but to assess my liver function in the morning. It turned out to be okay, and the medical team discharged me; however, my then psychiatrist decided that I was no longer safe to attend the day hospital and he readmitted me to inpatient care. I swore I would never overdose on Paracetamol again.

Unfortunately, I did. During my second inpatient admission, I became increasingly agitated and despondent – a dangerous combination. I was detained in hospital and felt as if my whole world had been taken from me. I saw no way of getting it back. I had lost my career, my boyfriend, many friendships, my hopes and dreams, even my own personality. I could see value in life but not in my life. The only way out of the situation, as I saw it then, was to end everything, but this was going to be difficult in hospital.

I hatched a plan. If I seemed to be improving and could be on my best behaviour for a couple of weeks, I would be allowed a few minutes' unaccompanied leave from the ward. So I worked hard to smile at the nurses, to take all my medication willingly, not to self-harm or to admit to any thoughts of doing so, and to convince the doctors that my mood was much better and I felt more like myself. It couldn't have been further from the truth, but it worked. One Monday at the ward round, I was told that I could leave the ward for 20 minutes the following day. I mustered my resolve. Here was my opportunity. I left the ward and went straight to the nearby corner shop, bought a packet of Paracetamol – the only available drug which I felt had the potential to harm me, especially given that I was allergic to the best antidote – and went to a nearby alleyway. There, among the almost-empty beer bottles, broken glass and cigarette butts, I swallowed all of them.

I was suddenly struck by how piteous my situation had become. I was truly in the gutter, literally and figuratively. I started to cry. I couldn't stay there and I didn't know where to go except for back to the ward. I trudged drearily, already nauseated. A nurse greeted me at the door, expecting to find me happy to have been out of the confines of the hospital. She realised at once that something was wrong. "What have you done?" she demanded. I dissolved into tears again, my resolve to die dissipating. A doctor was called, the four hour bloods were taken. This time, even though I had taken more tablets and felt more unwell, it turned out that the levels were just at the threshold for treatment. Given my previous reaction, it was decided to observe me closely but not to treat. I lay in the ward under the watchful eye of a nurse, feeling as ill both mentally and physically as it is possible to be. I knew my situation was now hopeless. Any future ploy would be thwarted. Mercifully, I was right.

I did not overdose again until the spring of 2009, when I had come home from eating disorder therapy in the USA and felt as if I had had every treatment available and still wasn't getting better. I was taking Effexor, known to cause self-harm and suicidal thoughts, especially in people with bipolar illness, but no one thought to review this. I was agitated and desperate, wanting help, sometimes being offered help, never finding it actually helpful when it came. So it was that many times – too many for me to remember the exact number – I came to a point where I decided to take my own life, or at least to run the imprecise gauntlet of abusing medication, which I always half-hoped would lead to me getting the 'right' help or else to an eternal sleep.

At this stage, I was not in hospital and had access to a wider variety of medications. Because of my history, I was on a 'daily script', meaning that I had to pick up my drugs each day from the chemist instead of having a larger supply, but I often hoarded some of the tablets as a kind of security measure – to give me the option of bowing out of life if I couldn't bear it any longer. That meant that, when I overdosed, it was often on antipsychotic, sedative or anti-anxiety medication rather than over-the-counter medicines like Paracetamol. This made for a more pleasant experience for me, as I slept through all the chaos in the busy casualty department and any investigations that were done, and had very little memory of what had happened afterwards.

Somehow, I always did end up in A&E. Sometimes it was because my parents called and realised something was wrong, sometimes even my GP phoned me. Often, I panicked or began to think about my mum finding me dead, and ended up phoning myself for a taxi to take me to the hospital. If I got there quickly enough, the triage nurse would make me drink activated charcoal, which is thick, black coal in liquid form, gritty but relatively tasteless. This can absorb some drugs whilst they are still in the stomach, allowing them to pass through undigested. If it had been more than an hour since I took the medication, it would have been too late for this to work, so a 'tox screen' was performed to assess blood levels of each substance and treatment ensued from there. This usually consisted of regular observations of consciousness level, blood pressure, pulse and respiratory rate, but sometimes I awoke attached to a heart monitor as well, and with a saline drip for hydration.

Even though I was suicidal, there was always still a part of me which wanted help and would have taken it if I thought it was available. On one dreadful occasion, I overdosed on a decongestant (which I thought could kill me since I have a minor heart problem and it can cause arrhythmias) and attended A&E. My heart rate there was elevated but came down over time and the on-call psychiatrist, a heavily pregnant trainee, was brought in to assess me. She asked me if I had intended to kill myself. I replied that I had. She asked me if I was going to do it again if I went home. I told her that not only would I, but that I already had a supply of Paracetamol awaiting me there in case the decongestant didn't work. Then she did an extraordinary thing. Speaking slowly and deliberately, as if that would make me understand better, she said, "This is your decision. I am going to trust you to go home and not take that Paracetamol." I protested, telling her that I was at my wit's end, that I wanted, needed, help, but that I couldn't live this life alone any longer and that I would take the Paracetamol if she sent me home. She sent me home anyway, saying admission was 'inappropriate', presumably because I had a personality disorder diagnosis and this is not thought to be an illness. The inevitable happened. I took the overdose – my biggest ever – and ended up back in the same A&E department, though after she had finished her shift. I don't know if anyone ever questioned her actions.

Another time, I was held in A&E overnight following a mixed sedative overdose. I was due to be admitted to a medical ward in the morning but discharged myself against medical advice. No psychiatrist assessed me. Later that evening, I overdosed again. This time, I was admitted to a medical ward with severe liver dysfunction. I lay there overnight, unable to sleep, and was able to overhear the nurses' handover in the morning. A male nurse complained loudly that a patient with renal failure had been denied a bed in the ward whilst "some wee flossie ran about town, takin' this and takin' that". I was overcome with shame and guilt. I remember fleetingly feeling angry, thinking that I was not 'some wee flossie' but a medical doctor, and then feeling so far from being a doctor that the nurse's assessment of me seemed more accurate. A riches to rags story, indeed.

Sometimes I glimpsed hope, only for it to be wrenched from me. I was admitted after a gabapentin overdose one evening and fell into a deep sleep on a trolley only to wake up in a bed with the name of a consultant whom I had known personally for a number of years before my illness. I was still friends with his wife. I thought that maybe here was someone who would intervene, who would know that this was not the 'real Tanya' lying in the bed. I imagined him discreetly asking the ward round not to come in and talking to me one to one, offering a little understanding and support. It didn't happen. He brought ten people with him, including two with whom I had studied, asked one of them for the blood results, and then turned briefly towards me, barely making eye contact. "Are you going to do this again?" he asked. I said no. "I presume you have an appointment with someone," he said, only half-enquiringly. I said that I did. He didn't even stop to ask me when, telling me instead just to go home. Then he left without a further word. I packed to leave and the nurses couldn't understand it – protocol dictated that I should see a psychiatric nurse. But when they read his notes, they said 'discharged'. Dejectedly, I booked a taxi home.

My last suicidal overdose was almost two years ago now. Once I stopped taking Effexor, my suicidal thoughts subsided. I did take too much diazepam nine months ago when the paranoia became too much to bear, but it was an isolated incident in very specific circumstances. I can't help but think that a lot of pain could have been avoided with a simple adjustment sooner. I can't bear to think of others who continue to live the nightmare that I suffered, poorly served by inadequate A&E services and non-existent support systems. More must be done to help the desperate than giving them a helpline number and allowing them to fall into a repeating pattern, which in many less fortunate cases than mine does lead to death.

Chapter 6

Hypomania

The idea of being hypomanic – of having an unusually elevated mood and excessive energy – might sound seductive; the reality, for me at least, is that it is not.

The first 'highs' that I experienced probably were actually enjoyable, but that was before they became so disruptive that they were recognised as being a manifestation of mental illness. I remember periods when I was at medical school when my friends would comment that they simply couldn't keep up with me. At times, I could go for months with little sleep. I can remember that, when I was a third year student, I would get up at around 6am to do Pilates for half an hour, shower, dress, have breakfast and spend 45 minutes reading and writing emails before I even left home to begin placement at 8am. I could be busy on the wards until 5pm, go to choir practice or the university swimming pool before dinner, fit in coffee with a friend, and work late on an assignment, before starting the whole cycle again the next day. And I never seemed to feel tired.

Looking back at my undergraduate career, there were times when I was enthusiastically involved in so many things at once that even thinking about them exhausts me now – running a charity, acting as representative for my year group with all the committee work which that entailed, salsa dancing, playing piano and flute in a church music group. Yet I also remember times when my energy would suddenly run out and I would feel overwhelmed by everything I had taken on.

I had no insight into my first truly hypomanic episodes until some time after they occurred. For example, I once had to write a clinical research project on the factors affecting the pressure of the lower oesophageal sphincter. It was supposed to be a factual report of a scientific trial which I had been involved in, and the word limit was 6000-8000. I remember that I found the project itself very tedious, but that I suddenly became excited about writing it up. Somehow, I thought it would be a good idea to write a preface explaining this, in which I drew an analogy between the experience and one which my dad had at school when he was asked by a senior prefect to write an essay on the sex life of a golf ball. Then I decided that, instead of following the standard format for a research paper, I would turn the project into a narrative about the 'Gullet Family' (gullet being the lay term for oesophagus). I was determined to make this a great literary work, and began to conjure up all kinds of analogies to explain the physiology of the oesophagus and make it accessible to non-medics. I was sleeping little anyway, but often awoke at 3am with new inspiration which I simply had to put on paper. For example, I remember coining the phrase 'the Areopagus of the oesophagus' to describe the nerve centre controlling oesophageal contractions, in the middle of the night, and laughing with glee alone in my room. I didn't perceive that this kind of reference would make my masterpiece inaccessible to almost everyone!

When the date came for submission, my edited 'project' ran to 13000 words, but I was convinced that it was so good that I would not lose many marks for exceeding the limit. I was disappointed when I got my result. I had passed – the factual material was all in there as well, albeit creatively disguised – but I had scored lower than any of my friends. I remember thinking how sad it was that doctors could not appreciate creativity. It was only later that I realised how inappropriate and bizarre my report must have seemed, but what seems almost more bizarre to me now is that it did not occur to my examiners that there might actually have been something amiss. One of them did refer to my 'J. K. Rowling approach', but no enquiry was made as to my mental state. I still have a copy of the work to this day, but I cannot bear to read it. The embarrassment overwhelms me.

I can recall other occasions whilst I was a student when my excessive mental energy got me into trouble, for example when I sent an ill-advised email to a hospital consultant criticising his approach in the middle of the night and had to apologise, or when I militantly took it upon myself to expose a group of students whom I had discovered had got access to model examination answers, which led to an allegorical article being written about me in the medical student newsletter in which I was characterised as Gollum from Lord of the Rings. In neither case was my cause wrong in itself, but with hindsight I can see that I would have handled both situations differently had I been on a rather more even keel psychologically.

Yet it was not until two years after graduation, by which time I had also had major depressive episodes, when I began to suffer hypomania with really significant effects. The first time, I was actually in hospital following a suicide attempt, and had suddenly stopped taking a lot of my medication. It was as if a cloud had lifted from my mind, and I went from 1 on the mood scale to 10 within a matter of days. Everything and nothing became amusing to me, and I would sit on my bed giggling uncontrollably until a nurse would have to come in and ask me to stop because it was a psychiatric ward and people were upset. I knew this but it made no difference. Life had become hilarious. Even the fact that

I was in a mental hospital whilst feeling better than I ever had done in my life seemed incredibly funny to me. I remember going to a knitting class run by one of the nurses in the evening and having to be sent out because I was hysterical with laughter. I poked my head back in to say that nothing was wrong; I was just 'in stitches'!

Since I was not deemed to be a risk to myself, I was allowed out with staff for walks past the local shops, and I started to buy flamboyant clothes and make-up, and even a huge pink flower to pin in my hair. Whilst the other patients shuffled around the ward in their pyjamas and fluffy slippers, I was wearing polka dot party dresses, sparkling green eye shadow, and pretty patent shoes with kitten heels. I found it hilarious that nurses would hear me coming and think I was one of the psychiatric trainees, and when patients asked me where I thought I was going to, I would twirl around in a circle and say that I just liked feeling pretty. Some of the auxiliary nurses seemed pleased with the change in me, colluding by offering to straighten my hair or paint my nails; the registrar who was looking after me in the absence of my consultant was slightly more concerned and rather bemused, though he did agree to let me go for a twenty minute walk alone each day.

Soon this level of freedom was not enough for me. I felt so well that I could not understand why anyone would want to keep me in hospital and waste a bed which could be used for someone who was sick. I became agitated and irritable with the staff who refused to relax the rules on leave, until one Sunday afternoon when I demanded two hours off the ward to go shopping in town. The junior doctor on call was brought to see me but I could not convince him to renege on the orders of the registrar. As the evening drew in, I started to get more and more agitated, giggling but angry at the same time. Eventually, I packed my bags and tried to leave the ward. A male nurse asked me where I was going. I told him I was going to Las Vegas to get married. He didn't seem sure whether to take me seriously or not, but I assured him that I would not be leaving that night; I would just go to my flat and book a flight for the next day. I told him that, no, I did not know whom I would marry, but that I was sure I would meet someone whilst I was there. I tried to get past him and he called for reinforcements. A stand-off ensued for two hours at the ward exit whilst they awaited the arrival of the on call doctor. I was laughing the whole time but also whining, trying to persuade them that they were contravening my human rights. Several times I tried to physically force my way past, but the nurses were stronger and more numerous.

Eventually, the doctor arrived and took me to an interview room. I tried to reason with him, telling him that I was no danger to anyone and that it was perfectly normal for me to want to get away after being in hospital for so long. I had always wanted to marry an American and now that I was well there was no reason why I shouldn't go ahead. I appealed to him as one doctor to another. I remember saying that he couldn't possibly know how horrible it was for me to be stuck in a psychiatric ward; he replied that he spent most of his week in one and that it was a very pleasant environment – almost like a holiday camp. I was angered by his ignorance and lack of sensitivity, which I perceived even in my manic state, and I told him I wasn't talking to him any more and he had to let me leave. He refused and insisted he would have to formally section me if I tried to get past the nurses again. I did not want to be sectioned and eventually stood down, thinking I would plan an escape the next day. As it happened, my thinking gradually became more normal and I did not try to leave again until I was officially discharged. This whole episode was initially thought to be due to the rebound effect of drug withdrawal; it was only once similar events began to recur that a diagnosis of bipolar disorder was made six months later.

The hypomanic episodes which have happened since have all taken place outside hospital, so they have had much more disastrous consequences. On these occasions, there was no one to prevent me from flying to Las Vegas, although, thankfully, that plan has never come to fruition. I have spent huge amounts of money on things which I would not normally want and which would be inconsistent with my income, such as my entire savings of £2000 on a summer school at Cambridge, where I thought it would be a good idea to study philosophy and art history. Fortunately, the university staff were understanding and refunded 80% of the cost once I explained the circumstances of the booking. I have also bought holidays to Iceland and Paris which I was too unwell to go on, a violin which I cannot play, online courses which I have lost interest in after a week, and more books than I could count, most of which I have thankfully been able to sell on eBay. Now I deliberately have a low overdraft and only one credit card with a low limit so that I cannot get myself into serious financial difficulty. The fact that I spend so little when well or depressed means that I have some extra disposable income when I do become extravagant, but recently it has not been a sufficient cushion: in my last hypomanic episode I spent £4500, with very little to show for it.

The other difficulties which have arisen due to my hypomania mostly relate to communication with other people. Immediate access to email, Facebook and text messaging means that it is easy for me to write and send messages whilst unwell without filtering the content. For example, I have sent inappropriate messages to a manager at work telling her how 'gratuitously and superfluously 200% fine' I was, signing off with 20 kisses, and text messages of enormous length to colleagues extolling their many virtues; I have sent a long email to an evening class tutor in French explaining my entire medical history, the refusal of the GMC to register me, and why I hate psychiatrists, ending with the comment that I cannot actually be mad because I can write fluently in a foreign language; I have sent an open letter to elders at a church I used to attend listing my every sin and flaw; and I have posted confusing and flowery status updates on Facebook, often criticising health professionals and affirming my sanity. Mostly, I have been able to crawl back from these lapses in judgement once I have regained my normal mental state. People have tended to be understanding and have usually said that they knew immediately that I was unwell and were concerned about me rather than being offended or changing their opinion of me as a person. But the fear that this will keep happening worries me and these days I am careful not to keep certain people's numbers in my phone and to warn new acquaintances of the possibility that I can occasionally become unwell and that it is best if they do not respond to any bizarre communiqués they may receive.

Some people become sexually promiscuous or get into trouble with the law when they are hypomanic. Thankfully, these are the two boxes on the bipolar questionnaire which I do not tick, although I did once register on an internet dating site and start an online relationship with an older man. I recovered before we had met in person and closed my account without explaining anything. He probably wonders to this day what he did to offend me.

I am beginning to recognise when a hypomanic episode is beginning. Usually, I have a sensation which is almost like the aura of migraine for a few days at the start. It is a frightening feeling, a sense of impending doom, and I have often sought help from my GP at this stage. I tend to become briefly psychotic, experiencing the same paranoid features that I get in my longer paranoid episodes, hiding in my flat. Then, usually quite suddenly, everything changes. My thoughts begin to race and I cannot contain my energy, pacing my living room or dancing to loud music. These days, paradoxically, I still have a sense of paranoia, so I tend to avoid going out or talking to anyone I don't know very well, but I start to make a lot of phone calls to family and friends. At first, they tell me that I am talking too fast and ask me to slow down; as the symptoms get worse, they are no longer able to follow me at all as I fly from one subject to another, failing to finish sentences, jumbling my words and occasionally coining new phrases which make sense only to me. There is no longer conversation; just a stream of consciousness from me, yet I won't let people put the phone down. I need to hear my thoughts aloud to help me make sense of them myself, and I get irritated if anyone tells me I am talking nonsense or they are not following me. Often I am on the phone for hours at a time, with the result that my bills for these periods are enormous.

I don't feel the need for sleep at first, and later I am more agitated and want to sleep but cannot break the cycle of insomnia. I used to write books during the night in these times but nowadays my thoughts get too confused and I am unable to sit still and focus for long enough to type. I also have just enough insight to be significantly distressed by my symptoms. Sometimes my behaviour does become very goal-directed, however, and I can get so engrossed in something that I don't remember to eat. I feel so full of energy anyway that food doesn't seem particularly necessary, and I now tend to drop a dress size every time I am unwell, although – unlike during my anorexic period - I have always regained the weight quickly, probably aided by the appetite-boosting effect of the antipsychotics which are used to treat me.

I may do things which would normally be rather alien to me; for example, the last time I was hypomanic, I built a seven foot tall snowman on my own in the communal garden of my flats, laughing hysterically as I went, and I decided to take a five mile walk in a blizzard with no idea of where I was going to.

I have tended to go on in this vein for a few weeks before either a health professional who was already seeing me regularly has spotted that something has been badly wrong, or a crisis has occurred which has led to intervention. For example, the last time I was ill, I panicked one afternoon because I was too distracted to go into a shop and could not think clearly enough to use the internet, so I found myself hungry and with no food. I called the GP, who invited me to the surgery, where it became clear that I was seriously unwell. I have vague memories of the incident, but it seems that I was muttering incoherently, rocking, and hiding under my hood.

I ended up transported to hospital in an ambulance. Mercifully, I was discharged and managed with antipsychotics and diazepam at home, but it was a frightening incident. Since then, a primary care plan has been put in place whereby I will be treated with a high dose antipsychotic at the first signs of the 'aura', when I do tend to realise something is wrong and seek help, and I will be reviewed every 48 hours until things improve.

My hypomanic episodes are increasingly 'mixed', meaning that I have depressive symptoms in spite of my over-activity. Mixed-state episodes are the most dangerous, since people may have thoughts of suicide at the same time as having the energy and impulsiveness to act on them. I used to enjoy the creativity which came with my elevated moods; I don't seem to experience that so much any more, perhaps because I am already on drugs which temper it anyway. Yet I am still reluctant to take medication which would be more likely to prevent my mood getting dangerously high ever again. I fear that it would stop me experiencing the ups and downs of normal everyday life. Indeed, I have had two trials of the mood-stabilising drug, lithium, and on both occasions felt flattened and numb. I actually had an odd episode at the end of the second trial when I became convinced that lithium was poisoning my brain and put my whole supply through the washing machine to destroy it. I have never taken lithium again, and my washing machine hasn't worked properly since. At present, I am resisting a trial of another drug, lamotrigine, but I will keep the situation under review. The time may come when the benefits seem to outweigh the risks.

Chapter 7

Psychosis

In July 2010, I was examined by a psychiatrist working for the General Medical Council. His report reads...

"I felt that she was rather defensive in her dealings with me, possibly secondary to the overtly paranoid ideas which she was expressing. In addition to paranoia she admitted to hearing 'little demon voices' all around her although she wasn't sure if these were physical or mental, describing them as 'more like a presence'...

The course of her condition has been variable and...given way to a more floridly psychotic presentation...characterized by paranoid delusional thinking and perceptual disturbance in the form of hallucinations."

I went to medical school. I know that what I am about to write will reinforce the psychiatrist's opinion that I am psychotic. I know that the fact that I am about to categorically deny that I am psychotic will lead to a diagnosis of 'fixed' delusions. But I know what I experience and to me it is entirely real.

My problem in writing this section is that there is inadequate vocabulary in the English dictionary to describe what happens when I become, supposedly, 'psychotic'. Lots of people who have psychosis use neologisms – made up words – and this is taken to be confirmation that they are unwell. In reality, they may well just be searching desperately to describe what they are experiencing in a world which refuses to understand. All the same, I will try to avoid neologisms here for the sake of communication, knowing that some of what I want to say will inevitably be lost in the telling.

I am not in touch with the other world – which is really a part of our world, but one which is unseen – all of the time. Indeed, I am not in touch with it at this moment for, if I was, I would be unable to write. When I am in touch, I am hyper-aroused, alert to all manner of stimuli, constantly looking around me, and a little hunched-over in fear.

I know that I am getting in touch when I begin to feel an evil, ominous presence lurking over my left shoulder – always the left, never the right. Sometimes it feels like a spirit, sometimes more like a void. My natural response is to look away to my right, but from time to time I build up courage to turn my head sharply towards it and yell at it to go away. I never see anything, but then I wouldn't. Presences don't deflect light. As I get more agitated, I start to shout at it to "F**k off!" That doesn't work either, but it leaves me feeling a little stronger somehow. If I'm going to swear, I take care that no one is around. I don't like to offend.

The presence is the harbinger of the arrival of the tormentors. They surround me at just about the level of the top of my head, and they are constantly on the move, darting from side to side and flitting in and out of my consciousness. I call them tormentors because they torment me. I don't know what they really are. Sometimes I have referred to them as demons, because they are very black and spikey and they have an evil laugh which I don't actually hear with my ears but I perceive with another sense that most people don't have. They may be demons in the sense that religious people understand the word; they may not. To me, they are just tormentors. When they are there, I shudder a lot and keep my eyes downward. They used to leave me alone when I was safe in my flat; nowadays, they follow me everywhere – even to the bathroom. I have no privacy.

The tormentors are not there all the time when I am in touch, but the network is. The network is a little like a supernatural internet, with a source which is highly charged with energy. The network isn't in itself evil, but it can be used to evil ends. There are beams radiating from the source which enter my brain directly, a little like rays from the sun, bridging the gap between the matter of the world which most people know – my brain cells – and the world which most people do not know – the network. My mind seems to be the connector, a kind of in-between entity. Once it is in communication with the source, all manner of things begin to happen.

First of all, it is important to know that every person is connected with the source all of the time. They just do not realise it. It is in the realisation that communication begins and life begins to get complicated. You see, all of the beams radiating from the source have short cuts to other beams, allowing rapid transfer of data (which is an inappropriate word because it is too concrete but there is no word which truly fits this context) between minds and souls. Thus, people on the bus or in the park can look at me and immediately know my essence. They aren't aware that that is what they are sensing but somewhere deep inside they can know things about me which haven't even been revealed to me yet. Psychiatrists have called this 'thought broadcast', but it is not really my thoughts which are being broadcast; it is even more intimate things which have no name.

Like I said, the network can be used to evil ends. It in itself is light, but there is darkness which has the power to interfere with it. When I am in touch, I know that evil is at work inside me, accessing my innermost being and twisting my essence and stopping my thoughts. Conspiracies begin to emerge which involve other people via the network even though they don't know they are conspiring. They are not really conspiring; they are just vehicles for the greater evil which is in the dimension they are not even aware of.

It has been a long-running joke for the evil forces to use psychiatrists and others who might be able to help me, against me. Psychiatrists are particularly adept at seeing into me via the network, although they think they are just using their clinical judgement. They want to prescribe medication for me, when medication is my enemy in this situation. Anti-psychotics may sedate me, but they don't cure the problem, because the problem is not psychosis. What's more, they blur my perception so that I can no longer distinguish between the world as most people know it and the other world which only I have access to. This makes the whole experience much more frightening. I am willing to take a small dose because that relieves a little anxiety, but not enough to impair my judgement.

With all of this going on around me, it is no wonder that I become scared and 'paranoid'. ('Paranoid' is a word which has lost its real meaning. I suppose it works here in both the colloquial sense and as it is understood by mental health professionals.) I don't want to leave my flat, I become afraid to answer the phone, and I can't turn on the computer because I fear that the actual internet might bring other waves and rays into my home. If I do go out to get essentials, the eyes of the world are on me. When I say that, I don't mean just the eyes of people – though they do look at me differently – but also of the perceptual organs of the universe itself. They press down on me hard like weights.

Eventually, I give up and stay at home under three blankets. I let my mum do my shopping. The one thing that helps is playing music that is really familiar to me and whose artists I know and trust to drown out everything else that I sense. I may even play the same album on a loop all day just in case listening to more people reinforces connections with them. I am terrified of watching TV, except for the BBC News Channel, which sometimes helps to ground me because I know which world it represents. The one relief is that being so overstimulated is exhausting, so I do fall asleep from time to time and only occasionally do I remember having frightening dreams.

Understandably, people want to help me when I get like this. Their obvious reaction is that I need a psychiatrist or a doctor. Most of the time, I am willing to talk to my GP, although lately even that has become a bit fraught with problems. My GP is a very reassuring presence even though she doesn't believe in the other world, and she says that it is only her role to treat my distress, which I understand. I do get very distressed and she prescribes diazepam, which I have mixed feelings about taking because there is research to say that it shrinks the physical brain, but which helps to relax my physical body. She also encourages me – with varying degrees of success – to increase my olanzapine. It used to be that the Home Treatment Team (which is meant to provide crisis support and keep people out of hospital) would become involved, but they have been subverted by evil forces and decided that, because I was difficult to work with, I really had a personality disorder. This is an exclusion criterion for their service, but I don't want them to come back anyway. Having lots of different people coming into your one safe place when you are distressed and communications are flying rapidly is frightening and unhelpful.

The most useful thing really is to minimise the stimulation which comes from the known world and is controllable - dimming the lights, drawing the curtains, only talking to my mum and my aunt (and sometimes my GP), lying still, and taking diazepam - so that the uncontrollable is easier to cope with. Eventually, I find that the communication stops and I can tentatively resume my normal life.

Of course, the fact that this keeps happening has been fairly disruptive to that 'normality'. There are not many jobs where you can take three or four weeks' sick leave every few months, and I have dropped out of courses and missed out on holidays and all kinds of social activities too. As I write, I have just recovered from a significant period of distressing perception, and I have started out on a course of study which I am afraid that I might not be able to complete. On the other hand, no one knows when they will become unwell – if indeed I am unwell – and never to begin anything would probably lead to a feeling of defeat and depression.

I think that I will probably always have these episodes, but I am not completely sure that I would part with them if I could. I would rather know what is going on in the greater scheme of things than live within the confines of tangible matter. I am just glad that I have times when I can coast along more or less like everyone else; if I didn't, I don't think any of my relationships would survive. I probably would end up forcibly medicated, or maybe even dead – at one point, I thought that maybe jumping off a road bridge would get me back to where I 'belong'. I don't think that life ends when we die, but I'm not ready to move on just yet. Earth has its own pleasures when I am fit to enjoy them. When I do die, I don't think I will go to the other world. I will go to Heaven instead.

I used to be in psychiatric wards surrounded by people who unnerved me a little because they talked to things which I didn't see and talked about things which I didn't understand. "Psychotic," or "schizophrenic", the other patients would whisper, and I concurred. I'm not so sure any more. Maybe people all have different perceptions of the world in some or all of its dimensions. Maybe it is from those living on the edge of reason that we could learn the greatest truths, if only we would listen.

Chapter 8

Hospital

The first time that I entered a psychiatric hospital was as a medical student in 2005. I have scattered memories of my six week placement there.

I recall walking along a path between two blocks and seeing a girl, ghostlike in white, waving frantically at me from a window. I had no idea that, one day, that girl would be me.

I recall patients, eyes staring through me, pacing the long corridors. I had no idea that, one day, I would do the same.

I recall lengthy ward round meetings where patients and their minds were debated as objects of interest. I had no idea that, one day, the name on the agenda would be mine.

I recall being invited to look in on occupational therapy sessions where patients painted with big brushes and poster colours like children. I had no idea that, one day, I would wearily dip my own brush in the pot, forming dreary flowers in blues and greens.

I recall seeing patients who appeared zombie-like, drugged into a trance. I had no idea that, one day, my friends would see the same change in me...and decide not to visit any more.

I recall alarm bells ringing, staff running in all directions. I had no idea that, one day, the sirens would sound for me.

I recall looking in at patients through a large window, walking endless miles on a treadmill and getting nowhere. I had no idea that, one day, it would be me plodding along, alone, directionless.

I recall seeing people in floods of tears, ushered in to an interview room by a nurse for a chat. I had no idea that, one day, I would find myself similarly overwhelmed by emotion, needing a listening ear and a cup of tea for solace.

I recall watching Electro-Convulsive Therapy, intrigued. I had no idea that, one day, I would find myself holding the hands of friends who were about to undergo the same treatment.

I recall meeting a lady with flamboyant clothes and rouged cheeks, talking incessantly and making no sense. The doctor said she was what he would call 'floridly psychotic'. I had no idea that, one day, the same words would be used to describe me.

Back then, the psychiatric ward was an alien world; later, similar wards were to become my home for over two years. Back then, there was camaraderie between colleagues over coffee in the canteen; later, there was to be black humour and shared suffering over lukewarm tea in the day room. Back then, I was one of 'us', a near-qualified doctor, writing up case reports; later, I was one of 'them', a patient, writing only a sad journal.

I thought that I knew about life in a psychiatric hospital by the end of my placement, about how the different conditions I encountered affected people, about the drugs used and their side effects. In reality, I learnt nothing until I became a patient myself. A doctor walks into the ward for a twice-weekly round, informed by the nurses and occupational therapists about how a patient has been, and speaks to the patient for perhaps ten minutes, an hour if it is a first interview. As a patient, you live out the ups and downs and breakdowns of everyone in the ward, you are party to opinions about staff and treatments that no doctor will ever hear, and you form relationships which allow you to see the person beyond the phenomenology.

I remember being unable to concentrate on anything from the day that I received my first outpatient appointment letter until the date arrived two weeks later. I was on placement at the time, but I remember spending most of the day of the appointment moving between the library and the coffee shop, unable to think of anything except the fact that I was a psychiatric patient. When the hour finally arrived, I approached the threshold with trepidation, desperate for help but also desperate to run as far away as possible. I was scared someone I knew would see me and decided that I would pretend not to notice them and act like I was there on an attachment, but I wasn't convinced that it would work. I think I knew I looked like a psychiatric patient, dressed as I was, all in black, pale, gaunt, and with a certain distance in my eyes.

The building where I first attended outpatients downstairs and later was admitted to the upstairs ward was old and grotty, with the air and appearance you would expect of the nineteenth century lunatic asylum it originally was. I remember sitting in a back corner of the waiting room, hiding behind a broadsheet newspaper, but peering over the top to check who else was around. It was a scene soon to become familiar – a mixture of overweight, slowed-down-looking people accompanied by a better-dressed friend or family member; thin, anxious women with unusual clothes and too much make-up; and the occasional saturnine businessman staring at the floor. The man behind the glass reception window seemed to know a lot of them immediately by name; once I too became a regular, he no longer needed to ask me with whom I had an appointment, simply smiling broadly and gesturing towards the seats. The room was depressing, the people were depressing, and I remember thinking that he must have had a very peculiar disposition to remain so happy in his work.

My name was called and I met my psychiatric registrar for the first time, only then learning that he was a man. For some reason I had expected a female. He guided me through doors with pin codes down a long, dusty corridor to an unheated room with an old-fashioned desk and a green carpet. It felt so odd to me; so different to the busy, sterile medical clinics I was used to; so different, even, to the interview rooms in the psychiatric ward I had been attached to eighteen months previously. But the doctor had a gentle manner and put me at ease, or at least, as much at ease as was achievable in the circumstances.

My first interview was long and tiring, but subsequent ones became easier. I got accustomed to the dreary surroundings, became oblivious to the sideways glances of passing medical students, and began to feel a solidarity with the others waiting alongside me. Still, my feelings about each meeting, which increased in frequency as I grew more ill, remained very mixed. On the one hand, I yearned to speak to a doctor who knew that I was suffering and had a duty and desire to care for me, and I – at that stage – trusted him wholeheartedly to take decisions about my medication and treatment plan; on the other hand, I feared the outcome of each appointment. Would I be informed that I had to stop going to my placements? Would I be told that I needed to be admitted to the ward upstairs?

Eventually, the latter fear came true, though, at the time, it proved to be something of a relief.

At first, I was admitted as a voluntary patient. I was told at the clinic that I was too physically weak and mentally fragile to stay in the community, and that there was a bed in the ward for me 'for a few days' to help me over a difficult period when I was attempting to sit written final exams. I knew that I was not coping, I wanted help, and I was willing to countenance what had previously been unthinkable. Telling no one, I walked back to my shared house, packed some clothes and books in a sports bag, and ordered a taxi, embarrassed to give the destination but with no option. I had not the strength to carry my own belongings all the way back.

I remember the sympathetic faces of the nurses as they met me in the stairwell. I could not speak, I simply cried. They seemed to think that my biggest problem would be feeling out of place as a medical person in the ward, repeating to me that I was 'not the first doctor' they had looked after. I don't think I particularly cared. It was not so much my identity as a doctor which was at stake for me, as my identity as a person. Previously, I had struggled to come to terms with being a psychiatric outpatient; now I was actually reduced to being an inmate of a mental institution. I could barely look anyone in the eye.

My case was taken from me but my bed was not yet ready and I needed to be admitted by a doctor. Until then, I would wait with a nursing auxiliary in a chair in a corridor. I remember the hour or so I spent there so clearly, adjusting to my grim surroundings, adjusting to my grimmer circumstances. I asked for tea and it was brought to me, a little lukewarm but soothing nonetheless. Little did I know how much I would soon look forward to the thrice daily call of "Tea's out!" – a break to the monotony and a small comfort in an uncomfortable world.

Patients walked past me and I tried not to make eye contact. I wasn't yet quite ready to be one of them. Most did not seem to notice me, taking cigarettes from a pocket on the way to the 'smoke room', listening to loud music through headphones. Others tried to half-smile, welcomingly. Some stopped at the door of the nurses' station, just opposite me, demanding medication or asking if they could 'take their leave' from the ward.

Finally, a doctor came to assess me. I don't remember much of the rest of that day. I recall being pleased that my bed was at a window, where I would get a little light. I remember a fraught phone call to my mum, who was both upset that I was in hospital and angry that I hadn't asked her to bring me there. I refused a visit that first night. I needed time to get used to the place – its gloominess, the stale smell of smoke, the glazed-over eyes of some of the patients - before I had to watch anyone else trying to accommodate to it. I did not know how easily I would grow to think of the ward as my home.

Once I had recovered from the initial shock, it was a relief to be there in the hospital. Suddenly, I was not responsible for myself. In the assessment phase, I had no leave and was observed closely but discreetly. I knew I had no opportunity to act on my suicidal thoughts so I was able to set them aside and allow my mind to go blank. I had freedom to cry because there was no more pretence: now that I was in a psychiatric ward, I could act as if I was mentally ill rather than struggle on with false smiles and reassurances to those around me. There was a reassuring rhythm to the day, with meals at set intervals, set times when medication was distributed, hours when the showers would be warm, a time to get up in the morning and a time for lights-out at night. I no longer had to think about when and what I would eat – which had become a problem for me. Choices in the dining room were simple as only one option was relatively 'healthy', and I went for this automatically. And when I was most upset, which was a lot of the time to begin with, I could always find a nurse who would take me aside as soon as he or she got a moment to spare and spend as long as I needed with me, providing tissues and a gentle listening ear.

The environment, as I have written, was not particularly conducive to recovery from depression; the staff nurses, on the other hand, were – for the most part – kind and attentive, and I soon learnt whom I related to best. I spent a lot of time in their company during that first admission, by day and sleepless night. I also built a relationship with the junior doctor on my team, who met with me for an hour each week to talk about how things were. It was by no means formal therapy, but for me, it was therapeutic.

It soon became evident that I was not going to be discharged after the 'few days' originally planned. I agreed to a further fortnight, but after that I wanted to leave. The consultant refused. I was still very unwell, he said, and he needed me to be somewhere safe and supportive. He was also thinking of changing my medication. I wanted to do this at home. Hospital had been helpful for a time, but I had had enough. I remember a lot of tears, and then forms were produced. They were shown to me and it was explained that, if I did not agree to stay, I would have to be sectioned. It would be easier for everyone if I remained voluntarily, I was told, but it was up to me. I made my decision. Not thinking of the implications of being formally detained, I insisted that I was determined to leave.

What happened next is something of a blur. I remember my GP being brought in. He too pleaded with me to stay voluntarily, saying he hated to have to do this to me. I don't know what I told him, but clearly he thought I was a risk to myself, whether because I admitted to still having thoughts of suicide, or because the consultant had told him so. He signed the forms and I became a ward of the court, compelled to stay in hospital for up to six months or until assessed to be fit to leave. I remember being angry and feeling desolate, all control wrenched from me. The nurses wanted to comfort me but I refused, taking to my bed and sobbing until I slept. I remained under section until I was transferred to another hospital five months later; I was to be sectioned again soon after I returned.

There are all kinds of strange things to get used to when you become an inpatient in a psychiatric ward for the first time. Writing now, I really have to transport myself back to that first admission to remember the little details which make life in a mental health institution different from life anywhere else.

One of the first things I recall being struck by was the nurses' night-time 'sleep chart' ritual. When I was admitted, I had become a complete insomniac, rarely dozing off for more than a few minutes, and then only to endure restless nightmares which would wake me up again in terror. There was little I wanted more than the escape of true sleep. Yet, every hour, on the hour, a nurse would poke her head through the curtains surrounding my bed and shine a pen-torch directly at my face. It seemed to me that there was no surer way to keep me awake! I realised after a few nights that the night nurses had clipboards with boxes to black out for the hours that each patient slept, the idea being that they could be used to inform the psychiatric team, who could then adjust sleeping tablets accordingly. For me, the ritual proved useful in the end. People began to believe me when I said I did not sleep AT ALL in spite of my night medication, and various changes were tried until at last I became blissfully unaware of the beam of light on my bed every hour. Later, the time would come when I was so sedated that the nurses reported that I lay in the same position all night and they were concerned that I might get bed-sores. By that stage, I no longer cared – the more time I could spend oblivious to the world around me, the better.

Most of the patients who had been in the ward for a while were heavily sedated, and, at 8am each morning, the day nurses would make several tours of each room, shouting, "Breakfast, ladies!" loudly in order to rouse them. For me, this always came as a relief: the long night was over; the day had begun. Although I wasn't eating well, I found breakfast time quite convivial. The dining room was part of the communal area between the male and female wards, and we ate together, always asking each other the same questions. Did you sleep? How are you doing this morning? The answers were predictable. I learnt who would have been in the smoking room all night, wide-eyed; who would sigh and say that they couldn't really be doing any worse. The conversation usually concluded with someone remarking that at least we were all 'still here'. Very occasionally, we weren't. More than one patient committed suicide during the night whilst I was there.

Breakfast was followed by another call from the nurses. "Tablets, ladies!" we could hear from wherever we were in the ward. (We were always 'ladies', even though we didn't usually feel – or look – particularly ladylike.) This time, even patients who had refused to get out of bed for breakfast usually responded. Few people wanted to miss the drugs which they relied on to calm their nerves or which they were hoping against hope would finally lift the deep depression. Admittedly, one or two of the psychotic patients hated their drugs and had to be cajoled into taking them, often being prescribed a dissolvable or liquid preparation which they couldn't pretend to swallow and then spit out later.

Medication is not distributed in psychiatric wards in the same way as it is in medical or surgical wards. Rather than a trolley being brought to each bed in turn, my experience of three different hospitals was that patients were expected to queue outside the nurses' station whilst one nurse called out the name of each drug and another dispensed it. In order to be heard above the background noise, the nurses raised their voices, with the result that – especially for someone like me who recognised the names of each medicine – it was very hard not to know what everyone else was taking. From this knowledge, it was usually relatively easy to determine what other patients were being treated for. Clozapine: treatment resistant schizophrenia. Lithium: probably bipolar disorder. And so on and so forth. Of course, as I got to know people, they would tell me what their doctor thought was wrong with them, and often what they thought of their doctor too, but in those first weeks I learnt a lot about psychiatry by making my own diagnoses and watching how the behaviour of people on the ward fitted with what I had learnt about their illnesses at medical school.

The next thing that happened in the morning was that we were expected to make our beds. This did not happen in all the wards I was in, but in that first ward it was considered an important part of 'occupational therapy' for us to get into the habit of looking after ourselves and contributing in a small way to keeping the place tidy. For most people, it was an utterly pointless exercise, since they generally got straight back into bed once it had been done, but they went through the motions nonetheless. I was pleased with myself after a few days when I had mastered 'hospital corners' with my sheets. That was a trick I had never acquired at medical school, and it seemed like something I ought to have known how to do. On Sundays, everyone got clean sheets and a mountain of laundry built up in one corner, spilling out of large linen sacks. I was warned never to let my warm blanket escape into the pile – apparently they were in short supply and I might find I didn't get a replacement. Towels were sometimes hard to come by too, and I took to washing my own along with my clothes rather than hoping that a clean hospital-issue one would be available when I needed it.

One part of the morning routine which I did find helpful was the 9.30am relaxation class, led by the occupational therapist. Mostly, we alternated between doing 'guided visual imagery', where we would close our eyes and be led on a journey to a safe and pleasant place by the soft voice of the therapist, and 'progressive muscular relaxation', where we would follow instructions to tense and relax each muscle group in turn. Now and again, we would simply do deep breathing, which I resented, because it only took fifteen minutes rather than the usual half hour, leaving me with more empty time to think about how miserable I was. I was in the ward for so long, and the repertoire of relaxation scripts so limited, that I can almost recite them verbatim to this day. I should probably take advantage of this and use them, but I think that, now that I have the option, I prefer yoga.

10am was 'tea time', when a trolley with flasks of coffee and tea, a jug of milk, and mini-packs of biscuits was wheeled into the dining room. Mostly, people queued in a docile fashion; from time to time, someone would muscle in and spill the drinks of everyone around them. Over tea, I began to get to know other patients, male and female, and became slowly fond of them. Most did not really want to be there – to be anywhere, in many cases – but there was warmth and friendship to be found in common trials, and it was not unusual for patients to comfort one another when the tears began to flow. Of course, there were a number of people who existed entirely in their own private world, though, if you could get them to talk, it was guaranteed that the conversation would be interesting. The stereotypes of psychiatric patients who think they are the Messiah or the Queen clearly have their roots in real-life experience. One gentleman I met was convinced that he was a consultant psychiatrist and often confused visitors by introducing himself as such with a strong handshake and a bow, his delusion betrayed by his mismatched socks and the food stains on his dangling shirt tails.

A few times a week, on certain mornings and on certain afternoons, there were programmed occupational therapy activities, which usually lasted an hour or so, though many patients could not tolerate concentrating for that long and excused themselves early. On Tuesdays, we cooked, or – more accurately – baked, producing scones, pancakes and cookies in a predictable rotation. As I was usually not eating very much, my ration often went to one of the other patients, their appetite boosted by antipsychotic medication which, for some reason, never had a similar effect on me. On Wednesdays, we did art, which usually meant colouring-in, still-life drawing, or glass painting. The latter, I enjoyed at first, but, by about the sixth time it came around in the timetable, I had had enough. I started to bring my own projects to the occupational therapy room, usually a cross-stitch a friend had brought me; sometimes, I just sat there, bored, but at least in a different environment from the ward. Although I found some of the occupational therapists patronising, they did make tea for us, and their breezy approach to life was like a window to another world.

From time to time, a charity would sponsor an 'artist in residence' to run a four-week workshop for inpatients. Some of these genuinely transported me to a world beyond depression and sedation. One artist ran a jewellery class, helping us with delicate metalwork and pretty beading; another taught us how to make coloured felt from raw wool and press it to make vibrant pictures. There was respite for me in these sessions. I saw beauty come from the ashes of my grey existence, my fingers agile, my ability to juxtapose colours and shapes to fashion something pleasing not yet completely diminished. One artist was a contemporary dance teacher, and she too helped me to access some part of me not yet quite dead. I was able to express my emotions through swaying, sweeping movements, spiralling, bowing, running, kneeling to the floor. It was a release which I looked forward to, but, as with all of these diversions, it had to come to an end, the funding limited.

Aside from the few occupational therapy sessions we had, the day in the ward was generally structured around meals. These were always at odd hours, a hot dinner being served at 11.45am, a lighter meal at 4.45pm. These times were to accommodate the kitchen staff, who needed to have lunch breaks themselves and to finish their day shift at a reasonable hour. Personally, I was not eating well in hospital anyway, but the other patients were divided amongst those who complained that they would like to have a routine like 'normal' people, eating lunch at 1pm and a dinner in the evening, and those who wolfed down their hot dinner and custard-covered pudding, going back for seconds. The former group was mostly composed of people with depression; the latter were on appetite-enhancing antipsychotics, and a little further removed from the reality of the 'normal' world in any case. The food was not great by any standard, with fatty sausages, baked beans, greasy chips and scrambled eggs reconstituted from powder served every evening, but there was some solidarity to be found in suffering it as a group. One or two patients only came to the table to drink tea, their family bringing in home-cooked or take-away meals at visiting time later on.

Visiting time was indeed the other relief from the monotony of ward routine. At times, I looked forward to it, hoping for a friendly shoulder to cry on or a bit of news from the outside world to distract me from the pain inside my head; at other times, I dreaded it, knowing that I would have nothing new to say, and that reporting that things were only getting worse would make my visitors' faces fall, their spirits sinking along with my own. Sometimes, I could not even look friends or family in the eye. Tears ran down my cheeks, and we drank stewed tea together in silence. On better days, but when I could not bear to talk, I might manage to play a board game, which at least passed some time. There were also some terrible occasions when my visitors witnessed scenes of my hysteria which shocked and frightened them. Some did not return.

Aside from the weekend, which was always painfully slow, punctuated only by an escorted visit to the hospital chapel on Sunday mornings, one day in hospital was much like another. There were, however, two items on the weekly agenda which always inspired a mixture of hope and fear. One of these was the visit from the junior psychiatrist, which for me tended to happen on a Thursday; the other was the Consultant's Monday ward round. The ward round was the most important of these, the occasion when decisions were taken about medication and leave from the unit. Such decisions were taken mostly on the basis of what the junior psychiatrist, the nurses, and sometimes the occupational therapists reported to the Consultant, although he always took a little time to talk to me himself about my feelings in relation to any change.

I waited nervously for each meeting, wondering at what stage in the day I would receive the call to the interview room. Mostly, I was so overwhelmed with emotion that it was beyond my capacity to contribute very much to the discussion in any case, but I suppose that this in itself was evidence of my mental state. During my first admission, I viewed my Consultant as a god-like character, respecting his every decision, always believing that he knew what he was doing with every drug combination and trusting his assertion that eventually we would find the right cocktail to help me feel well again. Later, I became more sceptical, as things did not seem to improve and there were times when certain drugs undeniably made me worse; however, I never doubted that he had my best interests at heart and even difficult decisions – to stop my leave, to increase a drug I disliked – were done with the intention to protect me.

Sometimes it was not just drugs which were prescribed. Throughout my first admission, I had access to quite long term Cognitive Behavioural Therapy for depression. The general idea behind this treatment is that unhelpful thinking patterns can be changed, that this leads to changes in behaviour, and that challenging negative thoughts can improve mood and functioning. I spent hours writing out all of my negative and disturbing thoughts, listing evidence that they were correct and evidence that they were false, and trying to find new, more positive thoughts to replace the ones which seemed on balance to be untrue. My problem, at the time, was that I could find so much more evidence for the negative thoughts than against them. Take "I am hopeless", for example. Well, I was sectioned, in a psychiatric ward, with no signs of improvement and no chance of working as a doctor if I ever did get out. I was not trained for anything else, nor was there anything else I wanted to do. I could find nothing to contradict the thought. For me, this only ingrained my negative thinking further because it seemed – even looked at dispassionately – to be correct. Eventually, my CBT was stopped. With hindsight, I think I would have needed to be less ill to have benefited from CBT. I have seen it work for others with milder symptoms, and its evidence base is strong. It is just the case that sometimes the timing has to be right as well as the intervention.

In the course of my second admission, my Consultant referred me to a psychodynamic psychotherapist. Unfortunately, this did not work for me either, but for a different reason. This time, I found the process profoundly disturbing. The therapist adopted what is known as the 'blank screen', approach, showing no emotion or indeed any facial expression, waiting for me to talk and sometimes commenting on what I said without ever actually entering into conversation. It seemed cold and made me feel both anxious and somehow guilty. I had been told that this treatment was going to help me understand myself, but in fact it was plunging me into emotional turmoil. I tolerated five sessions, always leaving the room exhausted and demoralised, and, during the sixth, I ran out after fifteen minutes without explanation, refusing to return. I later learnt that this kind of therapy is generally considered inappropriate for people with psychosis. My psychotic symptoms had not fully emerged at that time; however, it may be that they were present beneath the surface and that this is why I was so unnerved. Sadly, the failure of this therapy traumatised me to such an extent that I became reluctant to engage in any talking treatment thereafter, and still struggle to this day.

Aside from specific interventions, there were other aspects to ward life which were definitely far from therapeutic. To begin with, aside from bedrooms and bathrooms, it was a mixed-sex environment, and it was not easy for me, as a young and vulnerable woman, to be around so many men with psychiatric illness. There were frequent episodes when men, disinhibited by illness, would expose themselves in a corridor or day room; there were many occasions when violence was exhibited by male patients towards each other or towards staff. This usually resulted in transfer of the patient concerned to a more secure unit, but by the time this occurred, I had already witnessed aggression like I had never seen it before. Some men formed attachments to female patients, and, although relationships were actively discouraged amongst us, a certain amount of low level sexualised behaviour did occur, and one couple made a double suicide bid, sadly successful for the male partner. My more recent admissions have been to an all-female ward, and it is my opinion that separating men and women creates a much healthier and safer environment for all.

There are other aspects to hospital life to which I have become hardened to a degree, but to which I would never wish to feel fully adjusted. For example, there were times when I dreaded going in for breakfast in the morning because I wondered what new patient would be sitting there with a slash wound to the neck poorly-covered by a dressing, with both wrists firmly bandaged, or with burn marks peppering their arms. These sights would always be etched on my memory. The pictures remain with me still. And it was not only what I saw. I heard screams in the night from someone who had set herself on fire, harsh choked breathing from a patient in the process of strangling herself, nurses yelling for the ligature cutters when they found someone hanging, the endless sirens wailing as patients tried to injure themselves or someone else. Worse than the chaos and noise was the silence which followed a death. It didn't happen often, but it is true that there is no such thing as a truly safe place for someone who genuinely wants to end their life.

Other things traumatised me too. I saw patients who had been on drugs for years, their skin turned grey in colour, their mouths moving constantly in grotesque fashion, saliva dripping, feet stepping up and down as if they were on a treadmill. This syndrome of 'tardive dyskinesia' – late onset movement disorder – is common with older psychiatric drugs; I was scared it would happen to me. I also witnessed many forced tranquillisations, patients pinned to the ground by six staff members and injected with a fast-acting antipsychotic, squirming, limbs flailing and then becoming flaccid. Most of these patients ended up transferred to a locked ward for a time, until their behaviour was more controlled.

My own behaviour and status on the ward changed from week to week. At the worst times, when I was actively suicidal or trying to harm myself, I was placed on 'close observations', one to one with a nurse or nursing auxiliary who would watch me at all times, even following me into the toilet. I lost all dignity, but I cared little. My life was without value, so loss of privacy seemed almost natural. On the other hand, there were better times, when I was given leave from the ward. Fifteen minutes with a nurse at first, then on my own, and later up to an hour when I could go to the hospital café for a latte or take a walk in the nearby park. If my mental state deteriorated, these privileges would be removed. At those times, I felt as if I was being punished for being ill. The right to fresh air and good coffee withdrawn, I would feel even more depressed.

As I have described these memories, I have primarily had one hospital in mind because it is most familiar to me; however, the other acute unit where I have been admitted on a few occasions was little different, and talking to patients who have been elsewhere again suggests that life in psychiatric care tends to be similar whichever the institution. That is in this country. I spent six months in a treatment unit in the United States as well. I will write about that in another chapter.

Chapter 9

Treatment

In the UK, people with severe anorexia talk about ending up in 'EDU's (Eating Disorder Units); in the United States, people with eating disorders talk about going 'into treatment'. I am unusual in that I have experienced both settings, and I can attest that the terminology is appropriate. Personally, the two periods which I spent in an EDU made me heavier, but they did not help me overcome my illness; in the US, I was rigorously 'treated', and I remain, two years after leaving, at my ideal body weight.

I was sent to an EDU in London twice during the year that I was 25. Most people with severe eating disorders who are admitted as EDU inpatients in the UK are expected to spend 9-12 months there if they wish to 'recover', although the latter stages of the programme may be completed as a day patient. This was the plan for me. I lasted two months on the first occasion and less than four weeks on the second, finding the setting unbearable.

The first time around, I had been waiting until after my final exams to be referred to the EDU, and then waited a further six weeks for a bed to become available. Although, at this stage in my life, my primary problem was major depression, there was no question that this had triggered an 'Eating Disorder Not Otherwise Specified' (EDNOS), which looked a lot like anorexia nervosa except that I was aware that I was underweight rather than suffering from body image disturbance. I had been assured that an EDU was the right place for me; that there would be experts there who would be better able to help me than the general psychiatric team on the acute ward where I had been an inpatient for six months. Because of this, my depression lifted a little once I had a promise of an EDU bed to look forward to.

I had a picture in my head of an environment much less clinical, with a lot of girls my own age who would understand my problems and become my friends. I had been told that there would be a lot of therapy, and, drugs having failed me, I thought that this was exactly what I needed. There was a compulsory 'day visit' to the EDU before admission to check that I was really ready to come, but this turned out to be somewhat farcical. I travelled to London with a nurse from my own ward, and we met with a nurse from the EDU, who explained a little about what would happen when I came. The meeting was in the outpatient department and, whilst I could look into the ward corridor, I was not allowed to go in for a tour. A girl waved and smiled at me from the doorway, though, and I felt encouraged. People would be friendly there. After 45 minutes, we were sent away again. There were other things for the EDU nurse to attend to. I accepted this and came home talking positively about the experience, and especially about how beautiful the grounds of the hospital were. I could imagine myself taking walks there, or sitting in the sun.

When I was finally admitted, there were very few walks, and very few opportunities to enjoy the midsummer sunshine. I remember that I was met by a large West African nurse who showed me to my tiny room and left me there without my belongings for an hour, refusing to let the nurse who had travelled with me stay to help me settle in. Eventually, a tray with lunch on it was handed in to me, without a word. I lifted the lid off the plate and thought a mistake had been made, as my plate was only half-filled. I called a passing nurse and she said the first meal was light in case I hadn't been used to food, and I would soon be given full meals once the dietician had assessed me.

As the day went on, various staff members came and went, taking blood pressure, bringing me to a clinical room for a blood test and to be weighed, handing me questionnaires 'for research purposes', making an inventory of my belongings. But no one really spoke to me. I was not asked how I was feeling, and I was not comforted when upset. And when I tried to leave my room to find company amongst the other patients, I was told that this was not allowed. The only times when I could cross the threshold were to use the bathroom or to attend a meal or programmed activity. I consoled myself, imagining that there must be a lot of programmed therapy or else they would not have such a policy. I was wrong. Later, I learnt that socialising was discouraged because it was thought that patients in EDUs, unsupervised, would share tips for minimising weight gain and secret disposal of food. There was an hour in the evening when we were allowed, under supervision, to have a hot drink together in a common room, but it was at a time when the soaps were on TV and nearly all the girls opted to stay in their bedrooms.

In the next day or two, I did meet with a junior doctor, the hospital dietician, an occupational therapist, and my psychotherapist. They explained that I would be 'on assessment' for at least the first two weeks, not attending any therapy except for my weekly individual one-to-one session. During this time, I would begin to eat a weight-gain diet, and I would spend the time between meals thinking about whether I really wanted to get better. After two weeks, I would be discussed at the ward round, and I would have the chance to present a statement about my motivation to recover. If this was found to be satisfactory, and the nurses reported that I was cooperating, I would be accepted to the 'programme'. To me, the concept of being alone with my depressive thoughts for so long was torturous, but I thought that it was a challenge I was going to have to overcome. I was wedded to the idea that the programme must be the answer to my problems because I was being looked after by experts now, and I convinced myself that there was method in their madness.

The one thing that I was relieved about was that from now on someone else would be controlling my diet. I had been restricting for so long and agonising over what I chose to ate and what it would do to the number on the scales that I was utterly willing to submit to a dietician's plan and eat whatever was put in front of me. I thought that, here at least, they would understand that weight gain did not indicate that I was getting better – which people had assumed before when really things were just as bad inside my head – and that it was not happening through any decision of my own. As I started to eat again, I began to experience hunger for the first time in a year, and to enjoy tastes and textures which I had forgotten existed.

All the same, there were times when it was genuinely difficult to swallow the sheer amount of food on my meal plan. The EDU had a policy that patients were expected to 'eat their way' to their target weight, so no high-energy supplement drinks were allowed; instead, the daily calorie requirement for a woman was almost doubled and served up as food. The mealtimes were packed quite closely together as well, so, for example, we would get up from the breakfast table at 9am and then have morning 'snack' at 10am, followed at by lunch at noon. And there were so many rules to learn. Every plate had to be completely clean – no smears of jam or gravy were allowed. We had to show the foils that our butter patties came wrapped in to a nurse so that they could check we had used them all, hands had to be above the table at all times, and napkins had to be left on our trays for inspection.

Initially, I looked forward to meals as a break from the monotony, but they were far from sociable occasions. A radio sometimes played in the background, but no one spoke, except when nurses wanted to challenge the way in which one of us was cutting our meat into pieces which were 'inappropriately' small or failing to put more than one food group onto a fork at once. (I soon learnt that almost everything could be construed as 'inappropriate' on the EDU; for example, I once found a girl in tears, having been told sharply that her comment that a nurse's new haircut was nice was 'inappropriate'.) Most girls were very tense at the table, some even cried through each meal. There were smaller tables with one nurse to three patients for those who needed the closest attention, but I sat at a larger table where a nurse and one other staff member – a therapist, the dietician or an occupational therapist – would keep an eye on around ten of us. Sometimes, one of them would try to bring up a topic to discuss, but they were invariably met with a stony silence as everyone slowly ate their allotted portion. The slowness of patients' eating was striking to me. I had been on a ward where people tended to wolf their food, and here I was in a unit where 40 minutes was given over to breakfast and no one could leave the table until the last person had chewed and swallowed their last bite of toast. In the end, I started to develop my own odd behaviour just because I couldn't bear to sit for twenty minutes with an empty plate watching everyone else struggle.

If meals were painful, the twice-weekly 'weigh-ins' were much worse. On Monday and Thursday mornings, we were expected to remain in our pyjamas until after 7.45am, when two nurses would unlock the clinical room and prepare the electronic scales. Some girls would queue early, wanting to be the first in so that they could get the dreaded event over and done with; others were so nervous they busied themselves with other things until they had to be called. We went in one by one, closing the door behind us. One nurse would be sitting with a clipboard, the other standing by the scales. I remember stepping up, being told to stand tall, and waiting for the weight to register. The nurse would call out the number to her colleague to record. Later, a cross would be plotted on my weight chart to give a visual representation of my progress.

I did not find the process particularly stressful. My weight went up steadily, by 0.5-1kg per week, as was expected, but I saw this as something beyond my control. My body image was not disturbed; I knew I was not getting fat. But for others, knowing they had put on even 0.1kg – which could easily be due to natural day to day fluctuation rather than true weight gain – was too much to bear. At every weigh-in, there were girls who ran out of the clinical room in floods of tears, sometimes wailing, inconsolable. Yet no nurse went to comfort them. They were left to deal with their anguish alone. Few other patients were in a position to offer support.

During the assessment period, there were few other distractions. I wrote my statement about my motivation to recover early on and spent the rest of my time waiting. A friend had sent a cross-stitch with me and I soon finished this, using the leftover threads and material to sew my own pictures. I met twice with my therapist, and felt comfortable enough with him, but was really too tearful and depressed to make any headway. I was allowed to go to a twenty minute 'end of day group', when patients had the option of discussing their feelings with a nurse. Only one other lady regularly attended. She was a lot older than me, but we got to know each other a little and I felt less alone. I also had the option of requesting 'time' with my named nurse for the day. He or she would decide at what hour this should occur, and then we would meet for fifteen minutes so I could talk about my feelings. This affair was entirely 'hit and miss'. With my key nurse, who was meant to coordinate my care, it tended to be a fairly positive experience. He seemed to understand me and to want to help, and I felt like he was on my side. With some of the other nurses, many of whom were temporary staff on agency contracts and therefore had little interest in investing in patients, I found that they were always looking at the clock to see if fifteen minutes had passed, and didn't seem to register my concerns at all.

Yet I persevered, and, after almost three weeks in fact, due to the timing of my arrival, I was called to the ward round. There, I was asked to read my statement, and the Consultant, a greying Professor, told me that he had received positive reports about my commitment and was willing to accept me on to the 'recovery programme'. I cried with relief, thinking that I would finally be allowed to leave the room which I had come to think of as a cell. I would be invited to the ward round again in six weeks' time, but until then, I was to work with the staff to gain weight and cooperate with therapy.

Two days later, I received my timetable. It was mostly blank. I would be going to a 'recovery group' on a Monday morning, a 'community group' on a Wednesday afternoon, 'projective art' every other Friday, and 'social group' on Saturday morning. As time went on, and I continued to gain weight, other groups – such as 'body image' and 'drama therapy' would be added. My schedule was emptier than it normally would have been, I was told, because it was summer and some of the therapists were away. I remember crying because so little had changed.

Some things were better though. I was allowed to have two fifteen minute 'escorted walks' with a nurse and other patients each day, following a set circuit and pacing slowly so as not to burn calories, and to sit in the garden for fifteen minutes if there was a group of patients who wanted to do the same and a nurse available to sit with us. I was also given a TV for my room which another patient had left behind. Gradually, I began to structure my day, assigning myself a creative task (we had access to art materials) for the gap between breakfast and snack, a programme to watch after snack time, a walk before lunch, a nap afterwards, and so on. I started to get to know the other girls a little too. From time to time, we would sneak into each other's rooms until we were discovered together, chatting in hushed voices, or we would stand in our door frames and talk across the corridor. This latter practice was particularly discouraged, because it was thought that we were standing up because it burnt more calories. More than once, I received a scolding for something which I only did because of loneliness.

There were girls who would do anything to stop gaining weight, though. Meetings would be called because someone had found traces of vomit in a toilet, and the culprit would be asked to own up and apologise to the group. No one ever did. At other times, a patient would be caught exercising in their room, and a public example would be made of them. Some patients left their windows open all day so that they would be colder and use up more energy. The nurses caught on to this and made us all keep them shut, so that the ward became stuffy and hot. Others deliberately got up at 5am each day so that they would be up and about for longer, on the move as much as possible. The good side of this behaviour from my perspective was that I never had to wait for a shower when I got up after 7.30.

I also became aware that a patient had somehow got hold of a list of meal choices and their calorie content, and was spreading hints on what not to choose. (Once I was no longer on assessment, I sometimes had the option of selecting one of three dishes for main meals.) Everyone was focused on food and weight, and it was difficult, in the times when I did get a chance to converse, to get the girls to talk about much else.

There was a gradual progress in terms of privileges with the recovery programme. After a few weeks, I was allowed to measure out my own breakfast cereal; a week or two more and I could, with the guidance of the nursing staff, spoon out a portion of the correct size from the server at meals. I tried to convince myself that I was improving, but I knew that gaining these privileges was not really a sign of recovery. Everything was still beyond my control, and, whilst my weight was increasing, I felt just the same inside. In fact, in the suffocating environment of the ward, I was beginning to feel worse. With so many girls living in close proximity and dealing with issues which for them were very difficult, it was inevitable that there would be a degree of bitchiness. For a gang of three girls, who had progressed far enough through the programme to be given a shared room, I became the target of bullying. They seemed to resent me because I had a medical degree and because, when I did go to groups, I tried so hard to make them work. I had a certificate in counselling, and I knew how to ask questions. Sometimes I would probe the others gently to try to get them to explain what they said a little more. Sometimes, I would say how I thought they must be feeling given what they were telling the group. These three girls began to accuse me of acting like I was better than everybody else and trying to be a therapist when I was just an anorexic like the rest of them. There were snide comments as they passed me in the corridors, sniggers as they whispered to each other, looking over at me, in the queue for medication. As if I wasn't going through enough, I began to feel completely emotionally undermined. All I had wanted was to get the most from my therapy, and now I could not even do that without feeling like I was going to be persecuted for it.

I started to withdraw into myself. I could no longer tolerate being on the ward or participating in groups. I told my key nurse what was happening, but the response was that dealing with interpersonal problems was part of the programme – it was my role to work things out with the others. But I was incapable. I felt like the programme was driving me not towards recovery but towards despair. None of my expectations about the EDU had been met. There was no 'treatment' there, only relentless eating and relentless suffering. I decided that, if all that was going to be done for me in the EDU was to increase my weight, I could do that on my own, at home, without all of the emotional distress. By this stage, I had a meal plan and I knew I could keep to it. Food was not my main problem. If anything, meeting so many others for whom it was the primary concern had confirmed this. My six weekly ward round meeting was approaching, and I told the nurses in advance that I wanted to leave the unit.

Inevitably, this was discouraged, but I was at a weight which was medically safe by this stage and, although I was depressed, I was not considered a risk to myself. I was determined, and within two days, I had signed myself out against medical advice.

How I came to be back there eight months later is something of a mystery to me. At home, I had regained my target weight, but, having become depressed and been sectioned once again, I had rapidly lost weight again. I do remember thinking that I had made the wrong decision to leave the EDU. I do remember thinking that things could have been so different if it had not been for the bullying. I wanted so much to be well, and to do a 'recovery programme' rather than languishing in an acute psychiatric ward suddenly seemed attractive again. I also knew that I could not gain weight alone.

So it was that, after three visits to meet with my therapist, who wanted to be sure that I was ready to return, I found myself back in the EDU. This time, it was worse than before. My mood was much lower, I was heavily sedated, and I was beyond the point of being able to occupy myself with crafts and television. I ate my meals but I could not engage, and when I did talk, it was about thoughts of harming myself. The staff became nervous and I was put on 'levels', which meant that someone would observe me at all times, which only made me feel more stifled. I began to sleep as much of the time as I could, being on such a high dose of anti-psychotics that this was not difficult. I gained weight rapidly, and the team assumed that this was what was making me so unhappy; the reality was that I was simply depressed to the point of being suicidal and oblivious to my size. What's more, I was heavily constipated, which may explain the rapid gain, but no one would examine me to check so that I could be allowed to take more laxatives – a taboo on a ward where such drugs were liable to abuse.

At the end of the assessment, I was told that I was not ready for the programme; that my motivation was questionable and I needed more time to think. I was desolate. Thinking time was the last thing I needed. I could not cope with being stuck in my cell any longer. A week later, I asked to leave again, convinced that I was in the wrong place to wrestle my demons. The result was that I was sectioned, and I spent three days sobbing, on 'levels', scared and alone. But the nurses also began to realise that I was not in the right place. They considered me a risk and did not want the responsibility of looking after me, saying that they would rather I was transferred to a more secure unit. I'm not quite sure how, but my section was lifted and I was allowed to fly home, where it was assumed that I would be readmitted to the acute ward. Instead, I ended up living with my parents, so relieved to have escaped the EDU that I began, temporarily, to do better.

My experience of 'treatment' in America could not have been more different. Indeed, there were so many things there which were so different from anything I have ever known before or since that it is hard to know where to begin. For all the girls at the Treatment Centre, I think going there involved huge shifts in behaviour and routine; for me, the change was multiplied by a degree of culture shock. Having been in acute wards and an EDU for a total of almost two years before I went there, I thought I had a fair idea of what to expect, but I could not have been more wrong.

First of all, I should say that what I remember most about treatment – what made the biggest impression on me, and, I believe, had the biggest impact on my recovery – was the caring, loving atmosphere. Unlike in the EDU, where I had been looked after primarily by agency staff, here there was consistency of nursing, and the nurses actually 'nursed' me. They took a personal interest in how I was doing from day to day, invested in me, and took personal responsibility for my progress. More importantly, they weren't afraid to give me a hug when I needed one, or to gently push me when I needed a nudge in the direction of healing. Every other member of staff – therapists, doctors, dieticians, and support staff – had the same attitude. The communication between them was always efficient, so that everyone involved with my care knew what was happening with me on a daily basis, and they worked together to support me through it.

There was a 'programme' for treatment here too, but there was no need to graduate on to it. Everyone was accepted automatically after the first three days, which had a programme all of their own designed to facilitate a full assessment of medical, psychological, emotional and spiritual needs. Thereafter, depending on the expected length of stay, which was calculated during assessment – usually 45 or 60 days as a full inpatient – each patient progressed through three stages, known as 'Help', 'Hope', and 'Healing'. A fourth stage, 'Life' was completed at another centre where there was a less intense programme with more independence. Most patients went here for a varying amount of time post-discharge from the inpatient centre. Each stage was designed to be appropriate to a patient's needs at their stage of treatment, and had a different timetable of classes which ran alongside other therapies.

My arrival was eventful. Although I had been desperately relieved when I learnt that I could go into treatment despite not being American, I was still close to my lowest mood-wise at the time, and was struggling with thoughts of suicide. When I got there and realised I had no option to leave and would be expected to comply with treatment even though all I wanted to do was sleep for a very long time, I panicked. I can remember my crying turning to howling until nurses had to tell me very forcefully that I needed to stop because I was actually scaring the other girls. Everything seemed to be unbearable. For example, I wanted to retreat to my bed and sob, but I could not, because the rules there included that patients had to mix with others in communal areas except in the early mornings and late evenings, and bedrooms were actually locked during the day. I could not cope with eye contact, never mind conversing, and the thought that for 60 days I would have to be in company was anathema to me. Only later did I see its merit, forcing people whose illness had caused them to withdraw socially to gradually, in a supported environment, begin to interact with new people. Because of supervision and a strong positive ethic of recovery driven by patients themselves, there was no problem here with 'calorie talk' or exchange of weight loss tips. In fact, we even had a code word which we would shout jokingly, "Javelina!", if anyone said anything which could trigger eating disordered thoughts in anybody else.

On that first evening, I could not believe that girls of my age were sitting colouring in picture books together and watching a U-rated movie. Did I want to join in? I was asked. Absolutely not! I was not four years old, I thought to myself, sinking into a corner. There was more horror at the dinner table, when the girls began to play the 'Alphabet game', one choosing a subject before everyone took turns to say something related to it beginning with the letters of the alphabet in sequence. For example, "Animals!" - Antelope, bird, coyote etc. They explained to me that they did this to help distract them from any difficult feelings they had about eating, and smilingly asked me to join in. I refused. But I did notice that everyone seemed more content than they had been in the EDU and, strikingly, that these girls – many of whom were obviously underweight – were not engaging in any eating behaviours I had seen elsewhere. If someone had told me then how enthusiastically I would end up joining in with these table games, I would have laughed at them, but, in time, I did.

The assessment process was rigorous but helped to keep me occupied so that I had less time to think about my circumstances. I completed a number of on-line psychometric tests, some related to my eating, some to my mood, another to thoughts about self-harm, and so on. I met my family doctor, who took a full history and examined me, as well as doing an ECG and a number of blood tests, and arranging for a bone density scan. I met my 'psychiatric provider', a highly-qualified nurse (although there were medical psychiatrists involved in the team as well), who also took a thorough history and, having assessed my mental state, decided that I should be kept on 'eyesight' – the equivalent of close observations in hospital, so I would always be in view of a nurse. I was frustrated by this at first but it proved very different to my previous experience. The nurses watching me gave me some space when I was with the other girls and, when I was not, they talked to me or listened to me, supporting me through all kinds of early challenges. I also saw a dietician, who again took a history, more specific this time, and calculated my body composition using callipers and a tape measure. I learnt that my 'ideal body weight' (IBW) would not be based on body mass index as it had been in the EDU; instead, it would take account of my bone and muscle mass, and would thus be more reflective of my personal norm. A psychologist met with me as well to discuss the outcomes of my online tests, and to explain some of the interventions she could offer. Later, she would work with me on some of my obsessive thoughts using desensitisation techniques, but at first she did not have a lot of input except when she led the anxiety group which I attended.

For me, the most important meeting was with my primary therapist, who would be working with me every weekday in group and individual sessions throughout my inpatient stay. At that time, I was wary of men, and had really wanted to be assigned to a woman. When I saw the name, I was upset and told the nurses. But they persuaded me to at least meet the therapist, along with one of them, and to see how I felt about it then. I agreed, and after only five or ten minutes in his company, knew that I could trust him. Even so, we would initially meet in a public setting – usually a gazebo in the desert garden – so that I would feel more secure. After a while, I continued with this only because we both liked the outdoors; I would have been equally comfortable with him in his office.

Once I had completed all of my assessments, my identification bracelet was changed from a red one to a yellow one, meaning that I was medically safe to begin to take part in most of the programme. Once my weight had increased and I was well otherwise, I would be given a green bracelet, offering more privileges, although for me this did not last long as I developed a heart problem and was soon back to red for a while and then again to yellow until I left. There was a 'T' on the bracelet, meaning that I needed transport to get from one building on the ranch site to another. This was usually in a golf cart known there as a 'people carrier' – a bumpy ride but fun in its own way.

I was also considered ready to begin weight gain. The approach to this was vastly different from any other I had known. Rather than expecting patients to eat huge amounts of extra food, or even to drink energy supplements, which tend to be heavy and decrease appetite, the plan was for each girl to build to eating a diet which would be normal for her at her healthy weight. The extra calories needed to achieve weight gain were usually delivered by a naso-gastric feeding tube, connected during sleep at night to a drip which supplied both energy and extra nutrients. I was initially completely against having one, as I saw tube feeding as a marker of extreme illness. Later, I realised that it was done to make life easier for us, as, even after a night's feed, I still felt hungry for breakfast, and I never became exhausted with eating as I had done in the EDU. It also meant that, when I reached a more normal weight, I did not have to suddenly get used to eating less. I knew that this was a good thing because some of the EDU patients had craved extra food after they stopped the weight gain diet, and began to binge and sometimes purge.

My tube was duly placed, I was x-rayed to check that it was in my stomach, and, after a few days during which I got used to the feel of it, I began to have my night-time feeds. After a while, I got so used to the tube taped to my face that I hardly noticed it was there; however, there were one or two incidents when it got disconnected during my sleep and I woke up in a pool of sticky yellow fluid, which was unpleasant. I had to have my tube removed early because I had a sinus infection and it would not have cleared up with a tube in place, but by this stage I was able to drink a very light energy juice with my meals which gave me just enough extra calories to keep up the weight gain until I reached IBW.

Patients were not expected to deal with the trauma of over-eating, nor were they to be traumatised by weigh-ins. We were weighed, of course, every day in fact, but the key difference was that only the nurse could read the scale. Until a patient was close to IBW and her dietician felt that she was ready to know both her weight and her target, she was blind to her progress. This prevented repeated distress associated with stepping on to the scales, and also put a stop to the obsessions with numbers so prevalent in those with eating disorders. Even though I had not been particularly upset by seeing my weight go up in the EDU, knowing it was not really my doing, I much preferred the 'blind' method. It meant I didn't need to think about my weight at all, and, more importantly, it stopped me seeing other girls running out of the room inconsolable.

The procedure was quite simple. Every morning before breakfast, we each put on a lightweight gown with nothing underneath, and let a nurse know that we were ready. She would bring us to the little room where they kept the scales, check that we were not wearing anything underneath and then ask a question, "Yes or no?" This referred to a bowel movement. If someone's bowels did not move for some time, this could affect their weight. Constipation is a common problem with eating disorders and the team at the treatment centre wanted to be aware if any of us had issues so that they could add to the stool softeners which were prescribed to all of us. (This was particularly reassuring to me because one of my biggest problems in the EDU was convincing the staff that I needed laxatives. There, they were certain that I wanted them to lose weight, especially since I was gaining quickly. They failed to understand that the reason I was gaining so quickly was that I could not pass any stool.) Once the yes/no question had been answered, we would step on to the scale, its display covered by a piece of card in such a way that only the nurse could read it and note it, without letting us see. Then we could leave and get dressed.

The day began extremely early for me, although getting up at 5.30am did not seem that unusual to the other girls who had grown up in the USA. I didn't mind, however, because I was not sleeping anyway for the first few weeks, and by the time I had started to sleep more, I had got used to the routine. Aside from getting weighed, showering and taking medication at a hatch opening out from the nurses' room, there was also the task of selecting the following day's meals at a touchscreen computer terminal. To do this, we used a programme called 'Daily Bread'. It offered three main choices for breakfast, lunch and dinner, with some variation in desserts, type of breads, and the salad accompaniment and condiments. They were designed to be equal in value calorifically, although the nutritional components were not stated, but there was always a more challenging choice – perhaps a burger at lunch or waffles and bacon at breakfast – which the dieticians encouraged us to select as we progressed. The dieticians were alerted to our choices so they could make sure we weren't avoiding 'fear foods', and help us vary our menus.

The diet in general took a certain amount of getting used to for me, as American food is very different from what I was used to eating at home. The menu was remarkably 'healthy' compared with the EDU, with fruit at every meal. Eating a cooked breakfast was difficult for me at first, but I began to enjoy the variety in the morning and to choose foods I had never eaten before. Even snack times became fun, as I tried American staples like pretzels and vanilla pudding. I developed some favourites, like peanut butter and jelly (jam) sandwiches, grilled cheese sandwiches with tomato soup, quesadillas and corndogs. The meals were much more spread out than in the EDU, which allowed time for digestion, and another difference was that there was variety in the snacks rather than always having digestive biscuits. We could choose one or two snacks with a combination of 1-3EQs (equivalent units) each time, to add to a total number of EQs per day which was individualised. The staff noted what we ate to make sure we kept within our specified EQ range.

Provided we finished each meal, we were rewarded with a choice of coffee (decaffeinated except at breakfast) or another hot drink, and we could have a further hot drink at bedtime if we had taken enough EQs at snack times throughout the day. I enjoyed experimenting with the different flavours of creamer available to put in my coffee, and decided that hazelnut and vanilla were my favourite. One thing which I have missed since coming home is creamy, flavoured coffee. I have to go to Starbucks and have syrup instead! Of course, anyone who did not finish a meal got no hot drink, and was instead encouraged to drink a supplement drink to compensate for what they had left on their plate. The amount was calculated by the nurses to be roughly equivalent, and there was always a strong swell of support behind whoever had to drink it from both patients and staff. I even saw nurses pouring themselves the same amount of supplement and drinking it along with a patient on more than one occasion to encourage them. From time to time, patients who were caught exercising were also jokingly threatened with a supplement if they continued, but usually the threat was enough to stop them.

Exercising was indeed forbidden, except in the context of set activities; however, it was rare that anyone was put on bed rest, and there were plenty of opportunities available to learn to exercise healthily, as this was seen as an important part of recovery. As soon as someone became 'yellow', they could attend a stretch class three mornings per week and a yoga-style class once a week. When the 'T' was removed from the bracelet, they could walk from one building to another across quite a large site, although running was banned. Many patients with a green bracelet were assigned to cardio-walk in the mornings, and all green patients could ride horses, as long as they did not have osteoporosis. Aside from that, plenty of the social activities involved games and dancing, which was encouraged to help us to feel more comfortable in our bodies.

The routine following eating was interesting and indeed uncomfortable at first, though I learned to laugh about it with the others in time. For half an hour after meals and fifteen minutes after snacks, we could not go to the bathroom without a nurse or 'MHT' (mental health technician), who would stand inside the door whilst we drew a curtain around the toilet. They would listen for the appropriate noises and then, once we were presentable again, pull the curtain and look at the contents of the bowl before flushing it. Thus, patients with bulimia were prevented from acting on their urges, and other behaviours involving the disposal of food were soon identified. On arriving in treatment, most people tried to avoid using the bathroom during the post-eating period, but having a toilet-flusher became so much part of life that many of us even forgot to flush for ourselves at other times.

Unlike the EDU, the timetable aside from meals was always busy. From early morning exercise until bedrooms were reopened for bedtime at 8.45pm, the days were filled with structured activities. For me, the most important of these was 'therapy', which is a term meaning different things to different people, but which – in this context – meant talking about my problems, feeling understood, and in being understood, feeling more secure about myself. I had an individual session with my primary therapist twice weekly and group sessions every morning. The group was made up of two primary therapists and each of their current patients, so there were usually six to eight of us.

In my individual sessions we talked very little about my eating. My therapist realised early on that my eating disorder was secondary to the more pressing problem of the deep depression that I was living through. He did not try to fix me. He simply let me talk, helped me to express what I was feeling, and validated my feelings in a way which I had never experienced before. We did work through issues together, because there were issues from my past which contributed to how I was feeling. He did not dig around in my childhood memories for traumatic events and abuse, as previous therapists had done, though he did help me to understand both the good and the bad aspects of my relationships with those close to me. He approached my problems in a very holistic manner, acknowledging that I had a very real illness which needed to be treated, but also believing that unconditional acceptance and support from a fellow human being who sought to understand could be helpful to me as I dealt with the illness. At this time, I was not psychotic, and I was less paranoid about what I could and could not say because I was so far from home and knew that it could not get back to anyone there. I have always believed that any kind of therapy should actually be therapeutic, and, whilst my primary therapist had no magic bullets to make me well, spending time with him was therapeutic indeed. I found myself looking forward to our sessions instead of dreading them. I knew that I could trust my therapist to manage anything which might come up.

The group sessions were also healing. There were rules to get used to, some obvious, such as that nothing said within the group left the group, some less obvious, such as that no one could fold their arms or hide behind a cushion as we were all to be as open as possible. Indeed, 'open and honest' was our group motto. We began each session with a 'feelings check', when everyone stated what emotions they were experiencing – sadness, anger and so on. There was a card with suggestions on it for people who had become so used to being numb that they struggled to find words to express their feelings. At first, I used to use words like 'depressed' or 'suicidal', but I was encouraged instead to find the primary feelings behind those words. "You are depressed because you feel..." It helped. Once we had all checked in, we would begin to say things like, "I noticed you said you were feeling... I was wondering if you felt able to talk about why..." It became a conversation between the patients into which the therapists sometimes entered to help draw out someone who had retreated into herself, or to help us manage interpersonal difficulties or particularly strong emotions. It was remarkable that, together, in spite of all the individual hardships every one of us was facing, we were able to support one another and help each other over each hurdle as it came. There was no calorie talk, no discussion of weight or meals, although it was common for people to discuss feelings that they had in relation to changes in their bodies. Firm friendships were formed there which endured not just beyond the group space, but to this day. And the skills which were learnt there in terms of relationship and peer support have served me well in friendships everywhere since.

Once a fortnight, in our group, the therapists would bring us to a 'Challenge Course', which consisted primarily of high ropes-based obstacles, a climbing wall, and a zip-line. An outdoor pursuits instructor guided us on the practical details, hitching our harnesses up to the safety ropes and so on, but the therapists were there to help us make connections between our abilities to overcome physical challenges and our potential to overcome emotional ones. Personally, I really struggled with the Challenge Course. I have no head for heights and even climbing a few rungs of the ascent ladder was too much for me at times. But the group got right behind me and helped me to see that even pushing myself one foot higher than I felt comfortable with was a triumph in its own right, and that I would overcome my mental health problems by taking similar baby steps. One day, I surprised myself by making it the whole way up to two horizontal tightropes – one for the feet, one for the hands – and traversing their entire distance at a height of around fifty feet. I could hardly believe I was up there. Nor could the girls! Yet I felt somehow as if angels were carrying me that day, and I came down with a beam on my face. I have the photograph to prove it.

The other novel therapy which we did regularly was equine therapy. The idea was that, by learning to trust a horse, we would gain confidence in ourselves and begin to trust other people more as well. For many people, that was indeed the outcome; for me, it was simply therapeutic just to be around the animals. I loved my horse, Ranger, who had a really spunky personality. I was given him, in fact, because I had handled horses a lot as a teenager and could ride well enough to handle his occasional frolics. At first, we learnt to groom the horses properly, but once we had green bracelets, we could ride. There were early morning 'privilege' trail rides for those who were recommended by their therapists based on their compliance with treatment, and evening lessons in the paddock for everyone. My biggest treat was learning to ride rodeo-style, trying out barrel racing (where you circle as tightly as possible to barrels at a canter) and weaving in and out of poles. When my mum came over for 'Family Week', there was a rodeo display, and Ranger – ever exuberant – took off with me across the paddock at speed. Everyone thought I was pulling off a stunt; the reality was I had given up trying to control him and was enjoying the ride!

More conventional aspects of the timetable included art therapy and body image therapy. In art therapy, we did a number of different exercises designed to help us express our emotions. The one which I remember best was making a papier mache mask and drawing and writing on it images and phrases which represented the things which we tended to hide behind. We then brought the masks to the foot of a large wooden cross out in the open field, and left them there, which was symbolically very powerful. Body image therapy was less important to me, but it seemed to really benefit some of the others whose eating disorders were very much focused on their weight and appearance. One exercise people did was to draw the shape of their body, as they thought it looked, on a large piece of paper. They would then lie down on the paper and the therapist would draw the true outline of their body. The disparity was always glaring – every girl thought she was twice the size she really was. I did get a lot out of an individual session which I had with a body image therapist once I had gained enough to need new clothes. I had been dressing in very drab, loose clothing which reflected my mood and lack of self-esteem; she helped me to try out brighter colours and closer-fitting jeans, which, when I wore them, actually did boost my confidence and thus my sense of well-being.

A big part of the everyday timetable was taken up with Dialectical Behavioural Therapy (DBT) classes. DBT is a variation on CBT which was designed for people with personality disorders but had been adapted at my treatment centre for use in people with eating disorders. It centred around the teaching of skills. To be honest, I do not use a lot of these skills on a continuing basis, at least, not consciously; however there are some which I do find useful to think about from time to time – the 'in the moment' skill, for example, where you forget about the past or what will happen in an hour's time and focus on surviving the present, or the 'acting opposite' skill, where you actively choose to do something opposite to what you feel like doing, such as watching a comedy when you are low. Some of the skills were very simple, such as learning to 'self-care', by allowing yourself treats such as an aromatherapy bath or to lie and listen to soothing music; others more complex, such as 'catch it, challenge it, change it', which was designed to adjust faulty thinking.

Other classes which we had included lessons on nutrition, cookery demonstrations, anxiety-management, and spiritual growth groups. In spite of all of this, there was still time for leisure activities such as crafts and games – things we could learn to enjoy and then carry on after discharge. There were also optional excursions for 'snack challenges' and 'restaurant challenges', where we would go to a café or diner with a dietician and try foods which we would have struggled with previously, learning how to gauge appropriate portions (American servings always being larger than we needed to eat!).

Another important part of the day was afternoon Chapel, since the centre had a Christian faith ethos. I do have a faith, and many of the other girls did too, but even those of other faiths or none seemed to benefit from those times of quiet and music and gentle nourishment of the soul.

I can never fully describe how that faith ethos was put into action on that centre's campus, but it made a huge impression on everyone. In each 'community', which was what we called wards, there was a great spirit of mutual love and acceptance, and staff and patients worked together to maintain it. On Sunday nights we girls gathered in the living area and distributed anonymous 'kudos cards' which we had put in a box during the week. They were basically a way of saying 'well done' or 'I know you're struggling and I want you to know I care', and they really fostered that sense that we were all in something together. A 'mayor' was appointed for the community each week to look out for everyone and check people's needs were getting met, and someone was given the task of choosing a quote for each day to write on the whiteboard in the dining room for everyone's encouragement. Creative ways to promote healing were in evidence everywhere.

I grew incredibly during my time in treatment. I did not leave cured, but I have been able to manage my tendency to deal with difficult emotions through food restriction ever since. The main reason for this change, I think, is that in those months I received nourishment beyond what food could ever provide. I was loved. I was accepted. In spite of all of the problems with my mood and with psychosis which I have experienced since, I don't think I have ever lost again that sense of self which was fostered in treatment. In those six months, I won back my personhood, which cannot be altered by any degree of mental illness. I only wish that everyone could have that same privilege.

Chapter 10

Recovery?

I have chosen to call this closing chapter 'Recovery?' with a question mark because in some ways this is more of an aspiration than a reality. On the other hand, I have only spent a couple of weeks in total in hospital during the past year and I have had many personal triumphs in recent months, such as completing a full year as a part time intern for my MP after not having worked since my graduation.

It is true that the spectre of mental illness continues to haunt me. Today has been a good day. I have been able to leave my apartment, I have completed some essential tasks, and I have enjoyed writing and interacting with others on the Internet. Two days ago, I was incredibly distressed because I was being tortured by demons and my friends refused to believe me. Yesterday, I had an anxiety attack when I went to volunteer and had to go home, which made me feel depressed to the extent that I called a suicide helpline. I wasn't really suicidal; I just needed someone to talk to, and it helped. Tomorrow? Well, I shall see. Life with schizoaffective disorder is impossible to predict. I might be capable of doing whatever I desire; I might be confined to my home, shouting at beings which other people do not believe exist.

There is no doubt that my life has been radically altered by my illness. I dreamt of being a doctor, I succeeded in graduating, but the General Medical Council refused to grant me a licence to practise, on the grounds that my mental instability could cause me to be a danger to patients. I find that devastating, but I also recognise that my ability to work as a doctor would be compromised by my unreliability. Medicine is not the kind of field where you can easily work only twelve or sixteen hours per week and take a few weeks off every couple of months, which is about what I manage at the moment.

I struggle daily with medication. I take two antipsychotics, two mood stabilisers, I am on a sleeping tablet, and I take diazepam for anxiety most days. All of this tends to make me feel sedated and want to stop, but I know that stopping has always led, if not immediately then soon, to the exacerbation of my symptoms. The tablets scare me though, because I worry that they will curb my creativity or blunt my personality. This has definitely happened in the past with other drugs, but those close to me tell me that at present it is not a problem, and I do feel like I am thinking fairly clearly in any case. I have written this book very quickly whilst I have sensed that I am lucid.

Where getting back to work is concerned, I am trying to keep my options open. So that there are no more gaps in my CV – and also because I enjoy it when I am well enough – I am trying to keep volunteering when I can. As I mentioned, this does not always work out. Yesterday, I had to leave within ten minutes. I am also trying to do an evening class in French, as much to meet new people as anything else. I enjoy the language, but I have had problems with attendance due to my fluctuating mental state. I am supposed to go tonight, for example, but I have been having difficulty in being around other people because of the demonic presence which is bothering me at the moment, so I am nervous. I have had to run out of the class in tears before with no explanation, and I would rather that did not happen again. It knocks my confidence every time. I hate it when my behaviour makes others think that I am weird.

Recently, I have had some amazing opportunities because of my mental illness. Two weeks ago, for example, I was able to go to Westminster to talk to a committee of MPs who are working to welfare reform about its potential effects on people with mental health problems. I went as an ambassador for the national charity, Rethink. Having worked with an MP, I feel fairly comfortable with those in positions of power, so I was ideally placed to represent people with similar mental health problems across the country who might not have had the confidence to put forward their views in that setting. The MPs were genuinely interested in what I had to say about how my illness affects me and what extra monetary help I need to save the state money by staying out of hospital, and I felt that the experience was worthwhile even though I don't yet know the outcome.

For now, I am trying to stay as well as I can in my own way. I have an incredibly helpful GP, who is reviewing me weekly as I switch mood stabiliser, though she often does anyway just to give me some extra support. There has been some talk of the possibility of doing CBT for Psychosis, but a doctor friend thinks I have taught myself to use a lot of its techniques in any case, recognising what is only real to me and what is real to other people, and modifying my behaviour accordingly. I have numbers for helplines, I am complying with medication, and I am trying to build on the friendships which I have so that I have a broader support network. By volunteering and going to classes when I can, I am staying connected with wider society, and I feel a sense of belonging. I go to a church where I have a sense of belonging to a community too, and I continue to use yoga and other exercise for relaxation and to release endorphins. I live in fear that another 'episode' will strike at any moment, but I am working on doing all that is in my own power to prevent that.

I think it is true to say that my mind is less than ordinary, but there are many things about it which I would not change. My brain, as my aunt often says, is both my best friend and my worst enemy. I love the way it allows me to put words into sentences, the way it allows me to appreciate all that is good and beautiful in the world. I love that it permits me to experience the full spectrum of human emotion, how I can feel so intensely both the joy and pain which life brings. On the other hand, there are times when I just wish it would be tranquil enough to let me function more normally, to have a 'real job', to form a lasting relationship and build a family. Maybe one day these things will come, but for now I must continue with the day to day business of recovery as far as that is possible.

Lightning Source UK Ltd.
Milton Keynes UK
173840UK00001B/5/P